SUNSHINE SPANISH PHRASE

By

VICTORIA

PAPERFRO

Elliot Right Way Books
Kingswood, Surrey, U.K.

Made and Printed in Great Britain by
Hunt Barnard Printing Ltd., Aylesbury, Bucks.

CONTENTS

PART I

PART II

PREFACE

This book is intended to give a practical knowledge of conversational Spanish, and the phrases chosen should enable visitors to Spanish-speaking countries to express their everyday requirements.

Special attention has been paid to analysing the needs of tourist, holiday-maker and businessman. A feature of the book is the success that has been achieved in including every phrase likely to be needed by the traveller, while still featuring handy pocket size and great ease of reference.

At the very end of the book is a quick-reference section showing how to get help in an emergency.

HOW TO USE THIS BOOK

The correct use of a foreign language derives from habit rather than from knowledge. A person could know all the rules of Spanish Grammar, yet still be unable to speak Spanish.

The right way to learn to speak a foreign language is to memorise the most useful words and phrases which occur over and over again. These have been arranged in Part I of this book by an experienced language teacher. You have got to know these, so *learn them by heart by constant repetition.*

The second part of the book gives classified lists of useful vocabulary. Words closely related in sense have been grouped together under convenient headings to enable easy reference. The grouping of words in a logical, rather than alphabetical order, has been found more suitable for beginners.

There is no need to learn all the words in the second part by heart. They can be looked up when needed and combined with the phrases given in Part I. Thus the student who was memorising the Spanish for 'I would like to . . .', 'would you like to . . . ?' 'Where can I find . . . . ?', etc., has a stock of correct language forms at his command which he can enlarge as occasion arises from the lists provided in the second part of the book. He can further extend his vocabulary by use of a good dictionary.

SPANISH PRONUNCIATION

Follow a few basic rules and you will see that the Spanish pronunciation is one of the simplest to pick up from a book. It is what is called a phonetic language – every letter has its own constant sound, and is pronounced separately. Spanish has only five simple vowel sounds, which never change. Memorise these well and you will be happy to know that wherever these are placed in the word, the sound value is always the same. This does not make Spanish a monotonous language, as you will hear, once in the country, but it certainly helps us to master it with less difficulty! The alphabet has three extra consonants – **'ch'** (after C), **'ll'** (after L), and **'ñ'** (after N). These are widely used, and worth learning well. The guide to pronunciation below is by no means an exact reproduction of the spoken word, as no 'written sound' can be. It will however give you a pretty accurate base, from which you will hopefully perfect your accent when mixing with and listening to native speakers. This is the only sure way of picking up a true accent.

Vowels

These sounds should not be lingered over but spoken with brisk clarity.

Vowels	*Pronunciation*	*Examples*
A	like the English 'U' in utter, mutter	**para,** for **el mar,** the sea
E	like the English 'E' in egg, end	**depende,** it depends **la pera,** the pear
I	like the English 'EE' in see, weed	**vivir,** to live **el libro,** the book
O	like the English 'O' in Lord. Do not allow the mouth to widen and do finish the sound	**loco,** mad **el barco,** the boat
U	like the English 'OO' in spoon, soon	**la ducha,** the shower **la luna,** the moon

Consonants – (any not mentioned are as in English)

C	like 'TH' in thank, thought, when preceeding E and I. Instead of putting tongue in between teeth, place it behind top teeth to	**el centro,** the centre

	produce a slightly more hissing sound, like 'K' in key when preceding A, O, U	**la cabina**, the cabin **corto**, short **el cubo**, bucket
CH	like 'CH' in much, such	**el chico**, the boy
F	like English 'F' in far, fun	**la fecha**, the date
G	like English 'G' in got, game – when precedes O and A	**el gato**, the cat **gordo**, fat
	2. like a harsh sounding 'H' – try gargling your throat with no water – similar to Scottish 'CH' in loch – precedes E and I	**Gerona**, Gerona **el gitano**, the gypsy
	3. in combination with U and preceding I and E is like 'G' of got, game	**la guitarra**, the guitar **la guerra**, the war

Note: U is silent, except when written as Ü

	4. in combination with U and preceding A is like 'GW' of Gwenda	**el guante**, the glove

Note: There is no GUO combination in Spanish

H	always silent	**el hijo**, the son

J	like the Spanish 'G' which precedes E and I	**la jarra**, the jar
LL	Mixture of English 'Y' in yellow, and 'LLI' in million	**amarillo**, yellow **llamar**, to call
Ñ	Mixture of English 'N' in new, and 'NI' in onion	**el niño**, the little boy **mañana**, tomorrow
Q	always combines with U and precedes I and E when it sounds like English 'K' of key, kite. U is silent.	**el queso**, the cheese **quitar**, to remove
R	like English. When 'RR' occurs the vibration of the tongue behind the teeth is very emphasised	**pero**, but **el perro**, the dog
S	like English 'S' in sun, same. NEVER as in sugar	**el sol**, the sun
V	very soft, with a suggestion of a B at the beginning of the sound. In some parts of Spain, there is little or no distinction between the V and B	**el vino**, the wine
X	like English 'X' in extra, when preceding a vowel, and like English	**el éxito**, the success

	'S' in sun, when preceding a consonant	**el extranjero,** the foreigner
Z	like English 'TH' in thank, thunder	**el zumo,** the juice of fresh fruit

Note: **W** is not part of the Spanish alphabet, and only occurs in words with a foreign origin.

Intonation

(1) words ending in a vowel, or in the consonants **N** and **S** take a stress on the next to last syllable.
e.g. **verDUra** (vegetable), **LOco** (mad), **ANtes** (before)

(2) words ending in a consonant (except N and S) take the stress on the last syllable.
e.g. **venDER** (to sell), **longiTUD** (longitude)

Accents

There is only one accent in Spanish – a slanting line from left to right (/), which has two principal uses.

(a) to indicate a stress contrary to the two general rules above.

(b) to make a distinction in meaning of some words which are spelt and pronounced alike.

The accent *NEVER* changes the sound value of a letter.

e.g. **lápiz** (pencil) – the general rule requires the stress to fall on the last syllable (**laPIZ**) – the accent merely transfers the stress to the first syllable – **LApiz**

brújula (compass) – the general rule requires the stress to fall on the second syllable (**bruJUla**) – again the accent merely transfers the stress to the first syllable – **BRUjula.**

Note the difference of meaning in the following:

él, he	**el**, the
sí, yes	**si**, if
mí, me	**mi**, my
tú, you	**tu**, your
sólo, only	**solo**, alone

Note in the following how the accent indicates interrogation:

¿cuánto?, how much?	**cuanto**, as much as, whatever
¿cuándo?, when?	**cuando**, when
¿cuál?, which?	**cual**, which
¿quién?, who?	**quien**, who
¿qué?, what?	**que**, that
¿cómo?, how?	**como**, like

Question and exclamation marks

Warning of questions and exclamations are given by an upturned question and exclamation mark at the beginning of the respective sentences as well as the final mark.

¿.........?, ¡......!

TABLE OF THE SYSTEM OF IMITATED PRONUNCIATION USED IN THIS BOOK

(see also 'Pronunciation' P. 9)

ah (as in 'U' of utter)
ai (as in 'AI' of said)
ee (as in 'EE' of see)
oh (as in 'O' of copper, but with lips more rounded)
oo (as in 'OO' of spoon, moon)
N (as in 'NI' of onion)
L (as in 'LLI' of million)
tsh (as in 'CH' of much – note the slight T sound at beginning)
k (as in 'K' of key)
g (as in 'G' of got)
G (as in 'CH' of Scottish loch)
th (as in 'TH' of thank)
gw (as in 'G' of Gwenda)
Other letters are sounded as in English

SPANISH GRAMMAR

These briefs do not pretend to give a complete picture of the Spanish grammar; merely a few of the essentials from which you may grasp a general feeling of the language before your visit to a Spanish-speaking country.

Masculine and Feminine

In Spanish all things and people are expressed as masculine or feminine.

Masculine		*Feminine*	
el padre	the father	**la madre**	the mother
el hijo	the son	**la hija**	the daughter
el libro	the book	**la mesa**	the table
el coche	the car	**la puerta**	the door

He and She

El padre; él es viejo	the father; he is old
La madre; ella es vieja	the mother; she is old

El hermano; él es guapo	the brother; he is handsome
La hermana; ella es guapa	the sister; she is pretty

Like the nouns, adjectives are also masculine or feminine according to the noun they qualify, the adjective ending in 'o' for masculine and 'a' for feminine, e.g.

El perro negro	the black dog
La falda negra	the black skirt
El barco bonito	the pretty boat
La vista bonita	the pretty view

Note that the adjective always *follows* the noun.

There is no magic formula telling us which nouns are masculine and which feminine. The following rules however, with few exceptions, are a good guide:

Nouns ending in -a, -ad, -z or -ion are feminine and those ending in -o, -or, are masculine e.g.:

la botella	the bottle
la edad	the age
la calefacción	the heating (central)

la luz	the light
el vestido	the dress

Making plurals

If the word ends in a vowel, add 's'. If it ends in a consonant or unstressed vowel add 'es', and if it ends in 'z' change this to a 'c' and add 'es'. If it ends in 'es' or 'is', there is no change.

Look at these examples:

el libro	the book	**los libros**	the books
la cama	the bed	**las camas**	the beds
la luz	the light	**las luces**	the lights
el lápiz	the pencil	**los lápices**	the pencils
el rincón	the corner	**los rincones**	the corners

Note that adjectives and the definite article also take the plural form, e.g.:

la taza blanca	the white cup	**las tazas blancas**	the white cups
el médico joven	the young doctor	**los médicos jovenes**	the young doctors.

Indefinite Article (*'a' or 'an'*)

In Spanish this becomes **'un'** (masculine) and **'una'** (feminine) and the plural **'unos'** and **'unas'** (some):

Una silla, a chair	**unas sillas** (some) chairs
Una lámpara, a lamp	**unas lámparas** (some) lamps
Una chica, a girl	**unas chicas,** (some) girls
Una alfombra, a carpet	**unas alfombras,** (some) carpets
Un chico, a boy	**unos chicos,** (some) boys
Un cigarrillo, a cigarette	**unos cigarrillos,** (some) cigarettes
Un espejo, a mirror	**unos espejos,** (some) mirrors
Un árbol, a tree	**unos árboles,** (some) trees

Note that the plural of the indefinite article may also mean 'any' as used in the interrogative in English, e.g.

¿Hay unos chicos por aqui?	Are there any boys here?

Subject Pronouns and Verbs

Probably the most notable thing about the Spanish subject pronouns is that they are little used in actual conversation. Take for instance the verb 'To talk' (**Hablar**):

Yo hablo	I talk
Tú hablas	You talk (familiar)
Usted habla	You talk (formal)
Él/ella habla	He/she talks
Nosotros hablamos	We talk
Vosotros habláis	You talk (plural – familiar)
Ustedes hablan	You talk (plural – formal)
Ellos hablan	They talk (masculine)
Ellas hablan	They talk (feminine)

In spoken English we always use the pronouns. This is because, with the exception of the 3rd singular, the verb is the same all the way through, and the subject pronoun is our only method of determining the person ('I', 'you', 'he' etc.) in which we are speaking. Spanish is different. Look carefully at the above verb and note that each person is represented by a different ending in the actual verb which makes it unnecessary, though not incorrect, to use the pronoun as well. So, instead of saying '**Yo hablo**' – 'I talk', they merely say '**hablo**' – (I) 'talk' or '**hablamos**' meaning (we) 'talk'. This is the same in all Spanish verbs. The only subject pronoun best used is '**usted**' ('you' . . . . – formal), to distinguish it from 'he' or 'she' and as a mark of respect, particularly to older people.

So far we have used the verb **Hablar** (to talk) and seen how it is conjugated. Just to be a little more different, Spanish has *three* infinitive forms, as compared to the solitary English 'to'. These are . . . .ar (as seen in **Hablar**), ...er, and . . . .ir. ('To' is not translated in Spanish). Each is conjugated differently. Here are three verbs, each with a different infinitive and respective conjugations:

ANDAR (To walk)

Yo ando	I walk
Tú andas	You (familiar) walk
Usted anda	You (formal) walk
Él, ella anda	He, she (it) walks
Nosotros andamos	We walk
Vosotros andais	You (familiar) walk
Ustedes andan	You (formal) walk
Ellos/ellas andan	They walk

COMER (To eat)

Yo como	I eat
Tú comes	You (familiar) eat
Usted come	You (formal) eat

Él, ella come	He, she (it) eats
Nosotros comemos	We eat
Vosotros comeis	You (familiar) eat
Ustedes comen	You (formal) eat
Ellos, ellas comen	They eat

ESCRIBIR (To write)

Yo escribo	I write
Tú escribes	You (familiar) write
Usted escribe	You (formal) write
Él, ella escribe	He, she (it) writes
Nosotros escribimos	We write
Vosotros escribís	You (familiar) write
Ustedes escriben	You (formal) write
Ellos/ellas escriben	They write

Note the two ways of saying 'you' in Spanish. As in French, the familiar **'tú'** is only used when addressing small children, animals and close family. Out of this context it can be considered an insult not to use the more formal, though no less friendly **'usted'**. For convenience, the **'usted'** form will be used in the rest of this book. The abbreviations are **'usted' – Vd**; **'ustedes' – Vds.** With the exception of a few irregular verbs the above conjugations never change. Try practising with **CANTAR** (to sing), **BEBER** (to drink) and **VIVIR** (to live).

Note that 'it' is often not translated in Spanish:

Hace frío	It is cold (literally, it makes cold)
Son las diez	It is ten o'clock (literally, they are the ten)
Es muy interesante	It is very interesting

Question Time

There are two easy ways of turning your sentence into a question, each quite acceptable:

1. The first method needs no change in the original word order, merely a raising of the voice, e.g.

¿Usted vive aquí?	Do you live here? (literally, you live here?)
¿Usted habla Español?	Do you speak Spanish? (literally, you speak Spanish?)

   Note that the verb 'to do' is not translated.

2. For the second method you invert the verb, adverb, object with the subject, i.e. putting the subject last, eg:

¿Está contenta la niña?	Is the little girl happy?
¿Es bueno el hotel?	Is the hotel good? (literally, is good the hotel?)

Note that in written Spanish we are given advance warning of an interrogation by an upturned question mark at the beginning of a sentence; (similarly with the exclamation mark).

No for negative

To make a Spanish sentence negative simply place **'no'** before the verb. (Again, the auxiliary verb 'do' is not translated). E.g.

No hablo Español	I do not speak Spanish
No quiero vino	I do not want wine

Study these other negative words which can be placed after or before the verb:

(1) if a negative like **'nada'** follows the verb, **'no'** must also come before the verb;

(2) If placed before the verb they stand alone – only one negative can be used before the verb, except for emphasis, e.g. **No, no quiera vino.**

Nunca como pescado	I never eat fish
Nadie habla francés	Nobody speaks French
No creo nada	I don't believe anything (I believe nothing)

To be – two ways

In English we have the one verb 'To be' which expresses all the 'being' we need. In Spanish however, we come across two verbs 'to be' – **ESTAR** and **SER**.

ESTAR		SER
Yo estoy	I am	**Yo soy**
Tú estás	I am	**Tú eres**
Usted está	You are	**Usted es**
Él, ella está	He, she (it) is	**Él, ella es**
Nosotros estamos	We are	**Nosotros somos**
Vosotros estáis	You are	**Vosotros sois**
Ustedes están	You are	**Ustedes son**
Ellos, ellas están	They are	**Ellos, ellas son**

When first learning Spanish do not be too concerned about which verb 'to be' should be used. You will be perfectly understood either way, but try to keep to these guidelines:

ESTAR – used to express location, condition (health, emotions);

SER – used for everything else, particularly of a permanent state, ownership, fixed position, inherent qualities.

Look at these sentences:

Estoy en la Costa Brava	I am on the Costa Brava (location)
¿Está usted enfermo?	Are you ill? (state of health)
El coche es mío	The car is mine (ownership)
Paris es la capital de Francia	Paris is the capital of France (fixed position)

Order of Sentence

The word order of the Spanish sentence is largely similar to English and is best tackled in this way at the beginning, e.g.

Mi hotel es en la Calle Río	My hotel is in River Street
La mesa es grande	The table is big

Part I

HELLO AND GOOD-BYE

The Spanish are outwardly the friendliest people you could meet. However there is, amid all the kissing, back slapping and hand shaking, a certain code of greeting and leavetaking, with the handshake as the usual form of greeting between men and women. You will find that a peck on both cheeks is the general custom between women, whether on a first encounter or not. A firm handshake from a Spanish woman is rare – and is reminiscent of the days when every woman merely extended her hand for the gentleman to take and bow over. In many upper class Spanish circles this is still the practice.

The ways of addressing a Spaniard are varied and differ largely according to the situation you come across so that no fixed rules can be given or even appear to apply. The best advice is to address the person in the manner he has been introduced to you. With older people this will be either **Señor** (Mr.), **Señora** (Mrs.) or **Señorita** (Miss) and the surname, or **Don, Doña, Señorita** and the christian name.* As in English the young always use christian names amongst each other.

A simple 'yes' or 'no' without a 'thank-you', would be considered a curt reply in England. Not so in Spain – a short '**si**' or '**no**' is quite good manners. The situation naturally changes when you are addressed by a porter or waiter etc., who should follow his answer, as in England, with **señor** (Sir) **señora** (Madam) or **señorita** (Miss).

'good morning' or 'good day' is '**Buenos días señor, señora, señorita!**'
'good afternoon or evening' is '**Buenos tardes señor, señora, señorita!**'
'goodbye' is '**Adios Señor etc. . . .**' and 'hallo' simply '**hola**'

Note these abbreviations: **Señor – Sr.**
Señora – Sra.
Señorita – Srta.

*There is no translation of Don and Doña – they are merely a formal accompaniment to the christian name in more social encounters.

Hasta mañana	*ahs-tah mah-Nah-nah*	until tomorrow
hasta la tarde	*ahs-tah lah tahr-dai*	until this evening
hasta luego	*ahs-tah loo-ai-goh*	until later/see you later
hasta la vista	*ahs-tah lah vees-tah*	see you sometime (Lit. until the sight)

THANKS AND APOLOGIES

gracias	*grah-thee-ahs*	thanks
no, gracias	*noh grah-thee-ahs*	no thanks
muchas gracias	*moo-tshahs grah-thee-ahs*	thanks very much/ many thanks
usted es muy amable	*oos-taid ais moo-ee ah-mah-blai*	you are very kind
de nada/no hay por que	*dai nah-dah/noh ah-ee pohr-kai*	don't mention it
no importa	*noh eem-pohr-tah*	it doesn't matter
con mucho gusto	*kohn moo-tshoh goos-toh*	with pleasure (referring to something you will do)
es un placer	*ais oon plah-thair*	it's a pleasure
perdón	*pair-dohn*	sorry

Lo siento	*loh see-ain-toh*	I am sorry (Lit. 'I feel it' – to express a deeper regret or apology)
Lo siento mucho	*loh see-ain-toh moo-tchoh*	I am very sorry
Con permiso por favor	*Kohn pair-mee-soh pohr fahvohr*	Excuse me please
Perdón, ¿Cómo dice?	*pair-dohn Koh-moh dee-Goh*	I beg your pardon?
or	*or*	
¿Cómo dijo?	*koh-moh dee-Goh*	(in the sense of 'please repeat what you said, I didn't understand.')

APPROVAL AND DISAPPROVAL

Sí	*see*	Yes
No	*noh*	No
¡Bueno, vale!	*boo-ai-noh vah-lai*	All right! O.K.! Good
Muy bien	*moo-ee bee-ain*	Very good/well
Eso es	*aisoh ais*	That's it/right
Es verdad	*ais vair-dahd*	That's true
Es bonito	*ais boh-nee-toh*	It's beautiful
Estupendo	*ais-too-pain-doh*	It's wonderful
Es delicioso	*ais dai-lee-thee-oh-soh*	It's delicious
Tiene gracia	*tee-ai-nai grah-thee-ah*	It's funny/amusing
No está mal	*noh ais-tah mahl*	It's not bad
No es la verdad	*noh ais lah vair-dahd*	It is not true
Yo sé	*yoh sai*	I know
No sé	*noh sai*	I don't know

Comprendo	*Kohm-prain-doh*	I understand
No le comprendo	*noh lai kohm-prain-doh*	I don't understand
Me gusta	*mai goos-tah*	I like it
No me gusta	*noh mai goos-tah*	I don't like it
Por supuesto	*pohr soo poo-ais-toh*	Naturally
¡Claro!	*Klah-roh*	Of course!
¡No me diga!	*noh mai dee-gah*	You don't say!
Quizá	*kee-thas*	Perhaps
Si quiere	*see kee-ai-rai*	If you like/if you want
Me da igual	*mai dah ee-gwahl*	It's all the same to me/ just as you like
Creo que sí	*crai-oh kai see*	I believe/think so
Espero que sí	*ais-pai-roh kai see*	I hope so
Depende	*dai-pain-dai*	It depends
Es simpático	*ais seem-pah-tee-koh*	He is nice/kind
Una persona amable	*oon-ah pair-soh-nah ah-mah-blai*	A pleasant person
Es malo	*ais mahl-loh*	It's bad
Es horrible	*ais oh-rree-blai*	It's horrible

QUESTIONS AND ANSWERS

¿Va a venir?	*vah ah vai-neer*	Are you going to come?
¿Va a comer?	*vah ah koh-mair*	Are you going to eat?
¿Va a quedarse?	*vah ah kai-dahr-sai*	Are you going to stay?
¿Va a jugar?	*vah ah Goo-gahr*	Are you going to play?
¿Va a tocar?	*vah ah toh-kahr*	Are you going to play (musical instrument)?
¿Viene usted, verdad?	*vee-ainai oos-taid vair-dahd*	You are coming, aren't you?
Si, voy	*see voh-ee*	Yes, I'm coming
No, no voy	*noh, noh voh-ee*	No, I'm not coming

Note again how the negative is formed by placing NO in front of the verb.

¿Es usted francés/a?	*ais oos-taid frahn-thais/ah*	Are you French?
¿Está usted ocupado/a?	*ais-tah oos-taid oh-koo-pah-doh/dah*	Are you busy?
¿Está usted libre?	*ais-tah oos-taid lee-brai*	Are you free?
¿Está usted listo/a?	*ais-tah oos-taid lees-toh/ah*	Are you ready?
¿Está usted cansado/a?	*ais-tah oos-taid kahn-sah-doh/ah*	Are you tired?
¿Está usted casado/a?	*ais-tah oos-taid kah-sah-doh/dah*	Are you married?
¿Está usted enfermo/a?	*ais-tah oos-taid ain-fair-moh/mah*	Are you ill?
Usted es francés/a, verdad?	*oos-taid ais frahn-thais/ah, vair-dahd?*	You are French, aren't you?
Soy francés/a	*soh-ee frahn-thais/ah*	I am French
Estoy ocupado/a	*ais-toh-ee oh-koo-pah-doh/dah*	I am busy
Estoy libre	*ais-toh-ee lee-brai*	I am free

Note the feminine form given after the oblique stroke.
Note the two Spanish verbs 'to be' in use.

MORE QUESTIONS

WHERE? – ¿DÓNDE?

¿Dónde está él?	*dohn-dai ais-tah ail*	Where is he?
¿Dónde está mi amigo/a?	*dohn-dai ais-tah mee ah-mee-goh/gah*	Where is my friend?
¿Dónde está ella?	*dohn-dai ais-tah ai-Lah*	Where is she?
¿Dónde está el camarero?	*dohn-dai ais-tah ail kah-mah-rai-roh*	Where is the waiter?
¿Dónde está usted?	*dohn-dai ais-tah oos-taid*	Where are you?
¿A dónde va?	*ah dohn-dai vah*	Where are you going?
¿De dónde viene?	*dai dohn-dai vee-ai-nai*	Where have you come from?
¿De dónde es?	*dai dohn-dai ais*	Where are you from? (meaning origin, town, country)
¿Dónde es la estación?	*dohn-dai ais lah ais-tah-thee-ohn*	Where is the station?

¿Dónde es el ayuntamiento?	*dohn-dai ais ail ahyoon-tah-mee-ain-toh*	Where is the Town Hall?
¿Dónde es la oficina de correos?	*dohn-dai ais lah oh-fee-thee-nah dai koh-rrai-ohs*	Where is the post office?
¿Dónde son los servicios?	*dohn-dai sohn lohs sair-vee-thee-ohs*	Where are the toilets?

HOW? – ¿CÓMO?

¿Cómo va?	*koh-moh vah*	how's it going?
¿Cómo está usted?	*koh-moh ais-tah oos-taid*	how are you?
¿Cómo está su padre?	*koh-moh ais-tah soo-pah-drai*	how is your father?
¿Cómo dice usted?	*koh-moh dee-thai oos-taid*	what's that you say?
¿Cómo lo quiere usted?	*koh-moh loh kee-ai-rai oos-taid*	how do you want it?
¿Cómo se llama?	*koh-moh sai Lah-mah*	what is he/she/you called?

¿Cómo se llama este sitio?	*koh-moh sai Lah-mah ais-tai see-tee-oh*	What is this place called?

When enquiring about someone's health or well being, the following form, which is more colloquial, can be used.

¿Qué tal está su padre?	*kai tahl ais-tah soo pah-drai*	How is your father?

WHO? – ¿QUIÉN?

¿Quién es el jefe?	*kee-ain ais el Gai-fai*	Who is the boss? (also 'leader')
¿Quién es?	*kee-ain ais*	Who is it/who are you?
¿Quién es este hombre?	*kee-ain ais ais-tai ohm-brai*	Who is this man?
¿Quién es esta Señora	*kee-ain ais ais-tah sai-Noh-rah*	Who is this lady?
¿A quién ve usted?	*ah kee-ain vai oos-taid*	Whom do you see?
¿Quién lo dice?	*kee-ain loh dee-thai*	Who says that/who says so?
¿De quién está usted hablando?	*dai kee-ain ais-tah oos-taid ah-blan-doh*	Of whom are you talking?

¿Con quién está usted hablando?	*kohn kee-ain ais-tah oos-taid ah-blahn-doh*	With whom are you talking?
¿Para quién es esto?	*pah-rah kee-ain ais ais-toh*	Who's this for (lit. for whom is this?)
¿Con quién van?	*kohn kee-ain vahn*	Whom are they going with?
¿Con quiénes van?	*kohn kee-ain-ais vahn*	Whom (plural) are they going with?

WHAT? – ¿QUE?

¿Qué pasa?	*kai pah-sah*	What is it? what's going on? What's the matter?
¿Qué dice usted?	*kai dee-thai oos-taid*	What do you say? what's that?
¿Qué hace usted?	*kai ah-thai oos-taid*	What are you doing?
¿Qué come usted?	*kai koh-mai oos-taid*	What are you eating?
¿Qué bebe usted?	*kai bai-bai oos-taid*	What are you drink-ing?

¿Qué toca usted?	*kai toh-kah oos-taid*	What are you playing? (ref. only to musical instruments)
¿Qué tiene usted?	*kai tee-ai-nai oos-taid*	What have you got?
¿Qué dice él?	*kai-dee-thai-el*	What's he saying?
¿Qué hace ella?	*kai ah-thai ai-Lah*	What's she doing?
¿Qué comen ellos?	*kai koh-main ai-Lohs*	What are they eating?
¿Qué es esto?	*kai ais ais-toh*	What is this?
¿Con qué?	*kohn kai*	What with?
¿De qué?	*dai kai*	Of what/from?
¿Enfrente de qué?	*ain-frain-tai dai kai*	In front of what?
¿De qué está hecho?	*dai kai ais-tah ai-tshoh*	What is it made of?
¡Qué pena!	*kai pai-nah*	What a shame!
¡Qué tiempo tan ho -rible!	*kai tee-aim-poh tahn oh-rree-blai*	What terrible weather!
¡Qué día tan bueno!	*kai dee-ah tahn boo-ai-noh*	What a wonderful day!
¡Qué casa tan bonita!	*kai kah-sah tahn boh-nee-tah*	What an attractive house!
¿Qué día es?	*kai dee-ah-ais*	What's today? (lit. what day are we?)

¿Qué hora es?	*kai oh-rah ais*	What time is it?
¿A qué hora va usted?	*ah kai oh-rah vah oos-taid*	What time are you going?
¿A qué hora viene él?	*ah kai oh-rah vee-ai-nai ail*	What time is he coming?
¿Qué prefiere usted?	*kai prai-fee-ai-rai oos-taid*	What do you prefer?

¿POR QUÉ? – WHY?

¿Por qué dice usted esto?	*pohr kai dee-thai oos-taid ais-toh*	Why do you say that?
¿Por qué va usted tan pronto?	*pohr kai vah oos-taid tahn prohn-toh*	Why are you going so soon?
¿Por qué no?	*pohr kai noh*	Why not?

Note that **PORQUE** means **BECAUSE**: e.g.:

¿Por qué no quiere usted vino? – Porque no me gusta.	*pohr kai noh kee-ai-rai oos-taid vee-noh – pohr-kai noh mai goos-tah*	Why don't you want wine? – Because I don't like it.

¿CUÁL? ¿CUÁLES? WHICH (ones)?

¿Cuál? meaning 'which one' usually refers to a person or thing and is not generally used immediately before a noun, e.g.:

¿Cuál de las casas?	*koo-ahl dai lahs kah-sahs*	Which house? (Lit which one of the houses? – implying a selection of several)
¿Cuáles de los niños?	*koo-ah-lais dai lohs nee-Nohs*	Which boys? (Lit. which ones of the boys?)

¿CUÁL? ¿CUÁLES? meaning WHAT? or WHICH? is used only before the 'SER' (to be), e.g.:

¿Cuál es el primero?	*koo-ahl ais ail pree-mai-roh*	What is the first?
¿Cuál es la fecha?	*koo-ahl ais lah fai-tshah*	What is the date?
¿Cuál es su favorito?	*koo-ahl ais soo fah-voh-ree-toh*	What is your favourite?

¿cuál es esta?	*koo-ahl ais ais-tah*	which is this one?
¿cuáles son sus niños?	*koo-ahl-ais sohn soos nee-Nohs*	which are your children?
¿cuáles son los mejores?	*koo-ah-lais sohn lohs mai-Goh-rais*	which/what are the best?
¿cuál es lo más grande?	*koo-ahl ais loh mahs grahn-dai*	which is the biggest?
¿cuál es lo más caro?	*koo-ahl ais loh mahs kah-ṙoh*	which is the most expensive?
¿cuál es lo más barato?	*koo-ahl ais loh mahs bah-rah-toh*	which is the cheapest?
¿cuál le gusta más?	*koo-ahl lai goos-tah mahs*	which/what do you like best?

¿CUÁNTO? – HOW MUCH? ¿CUÁNTOS? – HOW MANY?

¿cuántos kilómetros?	*koo-ahn-tohs kee-loh-mai-trohs*	how many kilometres?
¿cuánto dinero?	*koo-ahn-toh dee-nai-roh*	how much money?
¿cuántos hombres?	*koo-ahn-tohs ohm-brais*	how many men?

¿cuánto tiempo?	*koo-ahn-toh tee-aim-poh*	how long? (how much time?)
¿cuánto vale?	*koo-ahn-toh vah-lai*	how much is it/how much does it cost?
¿cuántos quiere usted?	*koo-ahn-tohs kee-ai-rai oos-taid*	how many do you want?
¿cuánto pesa?	*koo-ahn-toh pai-sah*	how much does it weigh?

CUÁNDO? WHEN?

¿cuándo viene él?	*koo-ahn-doh vee-ai-nai-ail*	when is he coming?
¿cuándo vienen ellos?	*koo-ahn-doh vee-ai-nain ai-Lohs*	when are they coming?
¿cuándo van ustedes?	*koo-ahn-doh vahn oos-tai-dais*	when are you leaving?
¿cuándo vuelve ella?	*koo-ahn-doh voo-ail-vai ai-Lah*	when is she coming back?
¿cuándo vuelven ustedes?	*koo-ahn-doh voo-ail-vain oos-tai-dais*	when are you coming back?

Note: Sometimes **'¿cuándo?'** could be changed to **'¿a qué hora?'** – *ah kai oh-rah* – at what time, at what hour?

¿a qué hora salen ustedes?	*ah kai oh-rah sah-lain* oos-*tai-dais*	at what time are you going out?
¿a qué hora quiere usted el desayuno?	*ah kai oh-rah kee-ai-rai oos-taid ail dai-sah-yoo-noh*	at what time do you (sing.) want breakfast?

GENERAL QUESTIONS

¿puede usted arreglar esto por favor?	*poo-ai-dai oos-taid ah-rrai-glahr ais-toh phor fah-vohr*	can you arrange/mend this please?
¿puede usted decirme cuándo quiere comer?	*poo-ai-dai oos-taid dai-theer-mai koo-ahn-doh kee-ai-rai koh-mair*	can you tell me when you want to eat?

¿puede usted decirme si el señor B . . . vive aquí?	*poo-ai-dai oos-taid dai-theer-mai see ail sai-Nohr B.. vee-vai ah-kee*	can you tell me if Mr. B . . . lives here?
¿puede usted prestarme el bolígrafo?	*poo-ai-dai oos-taid prais-tahr-mai ail boh-lee-grah-foh*	can you lend me the biro?

COMMANDS AND REQUESTS

It is polite to add **'por favor'** – *pohr fah-vohr* – please, to each of the following:

¡pase!	*pah-sai*	come in/go in!
¡salga!	*sahl-gah*	come out/go out!
¡váyase!	*vah-yah-sai*	go!
¡márchese!	*mahr-tshah-sai*	go away/get out!
¡venga aquí!	*vain-gah ah-kee*	come here!
¡pase por allí!	*pah-sai pohr ah-Lee*	go through that way!
¡pase por aquí!	*pah-sai pohr ah-kee*	come in this way!
¡quédese aquí!	*kai-dai-sai ah-kee*	stay here!
¡mira esto!	*mee-rah ais-toh*	look at that!
¡démelo!	*dai-mai-loh*	give it to me!
¡hable inglés!	*ah-blai een-glais*	speak English!
¡hable más alto!	*ah-blai mahs ahl-toh*	speak louder!
¡hable más despacio!	*ah-blai mahs dais-pah-thee-oh*	speak more slowly!

¡tómelo!	*toh-mai-loh*	take it!
¡coja dos!	*koh-Gah dohs*	take two of them!
¡enséñeme eso!	*ain-sai-Nai-mai ai-soh*	show me that!
¡escúcheme!	*ais-koo-tshai-mai*	listen to me!
¡espere aquí!	*ais-pai-rai ah-kee*	wait here!
¡dígalo!	*dee-gah-loh*	say it!
¡hágalo!	*ah-gah-loh*	do it!
¡cuidado!	*koo-ee-dah-doh*	look out/be careful!
¡deprisa!	*dai-pree-sah*	hurry! hurry!
¡más rápido!	*mahs rah-pee-doh*	faster!
¡más rápido todavía!	*mahs rah-pee-doh toh-dah-vee-ah*	faster still!
¡siéntese!	*see-ain-tai-sai*	sit down!
¡póngase de pie!	*pohn-gah-sai dai pee-ai*	stand up!

DON'T!

When making a negative command, place NO before the verb and any pronouns. Object pronouns separate themselves from the verb and are placed before it.

¡no pase!	*noh pah-sai*	don't go in!
¡no salga	*noh sahl-gah*	don't go out!
¡no venga!	*noh vain-gah*	don't come!
¡no mire!	*noh mee-rai*	don't look!
¡no se lo dé a él!	*nòh sai loh dai ah ail*	don't give it to him!
¡no tan deprisa!	*noh tahn dai-pree-sah*	not so quickly!
¡no espere!	*noh aís-pai-rai*	don't wait!
¡no lo haga!	*noh loh ha-gah*	don't do that!
¡no les es diga nada!	*noh lais dee-gah nah-dah ais*	don't tell them anything!
¡no vaya!	*noh vah-yah*	don't go!
¡no toque!	*noh toh-kai*	don't touch!
¡basta!	*bahs-tah*	enough!
¡más!	*mahs*	not enough! (more!)

TRANSLATING COMMON WORDS

To Have – this is translated into Spanish by two verbs **Tener** and **Haber** – the latter being used only as an auxiliary verb (I *have* eaten).

Tener	*tai-nair*	To have	**Haber**	*ah-bair*
Yo tengo	*yoh tain-goh*	I have	**Yo he**	*yoh ai*
Tú tienes	*too tee-ai-nais*	You (fam) have	**Tú has**	*too ahs*
Usted tiene	*oos-taid tee-ai-nai*	You have	**Usted ha**	*oos-taid ah*
Él, ella tiene	*ail ai-Lah tee-ai-nai*	He, she has	**Él, ella ha**	*ail ai-La ah*
Nosotros tenemos	*noh-soh-trohs tai-nai-mohs*	We have	**Nosotros hemos**	*ai-mohs*
Vosotros tenéis	*voh-soh-trohs tai-nai-ees*	You (fam) have	**Vosotros habéis**	*ah-bai-ees*
Ustedes tienen	*oos-tai-dais tee-ai-nain*	You have	**Ustedes han**	*ahn*
Ellos, ellas tienen	*ai-Lohs, ai-Lahs tee-ai-nain*	They have	**Ellos, ellas han**	*ahn*

Uses of To Have

Possession

Tengo dos perros	*tain-goh-dohs pai-rrohs*	I have two dogs

Necessity

Tenemos que comprar peras	*tai-nai-mohs kai kohm-prahr pai-rahs*	We have to buy pears
Tengo que leer este libro	*tain-goh kai lai-air ais-tai lee-broh*	I have to read this book
¿Tiene ella que andar?	*tee-ai-nai ai-Lah kai ahn-dahr*	Does she have to walk?
¿Tengo que esperar?	*tain-goh kai ais-pai-rahr*	Do I have to wait?
¿Tengo que pagar ahora?	*tain-goh kai pah-gahr ah-oh-rah*	Do I have to pay now?

State of being

Tengo hambre	*tain-goh ahm-brai*	I am hungry
Tengo sed	*tain-goh said*	I am thirsty
Tengo calor	*tain-goh kah-lohr*	I am hot

Tiene usted razón	*tee-ai-nai oos-taid rah-thohn*	You are right
¿Tiene él dolores?	*tee-ai-nai ail doh-loh-rais*	Is he in pain (Lit. does he have pain?)
Auxiliary Verb		
¿Lo ha entendido usted?	*loh ah ain-tain-dee-doh oos-taid*	Have you understood it?
Lo he llevado	*loh ai Lai-vah-doh*	I have taken it away
Lo hemos comido	*loh ai-mohs koh-mee-doh*	We have eaten it
To Go		
IR	*eer*	
yo voy	*voh-ee*	I go
tú vas	*vahs*	you (fam) go
usted va	*vah*	you go
él, ella va	*vah*	he, she goes
nosotros vamos	*vah-mohs*	we go
vosotros váis	*vah-ees*	you (fam) go
ustedes van	*vahn*	you go
ellos, ellas van	*vahn*	they go

Voy a la ciudad	*voh-ee ah lah thee-oo-dahd*	I am going into town
Vamos a buscar a los otros	*vah-mohs ah boos-kahr ah lohs oh-trohs*	Let's go and look for the others
Ellos van al cine	*ai-Lohs vahn ahl thee-nai*	They are going to the cinema

Note: ¡vamos!, can also mean let's! –¡vamos a dar una vuelta! – let's go for a walk!

HAY	*ah-ee*	There is – There are
Hay una habitación libre	*ah-ee oon-ah ah-bee-ta-thee-ohn lee-brai*	There is one free room
Hay dos baños en el segundo piso	*ah-ee dohs bah-Nohs ain ail sai-goon-doh pee-soh*	There are two bathrooms on the second floor
¿Hay un señor Jones en el bar?	*ahee oon sai-Nohr Jones ain ail bahr*	Is there a Mr Jones in the bar?

Note: That 'there is' and 'there are', are both translated by 'hay'.

Some–Any (also Grammar P. 20.)

Aquí hay pan	*ah-kee ah-ee pahn*	Here is (some) bread
¿Hay carne?	*ah-ee kahr-nai*	Is there any meat?
¿Tiene usted cigarrillos?	*tee-ai-nai oos-taid thee-gah-ree-Lohs*	Do you have any cigarettes?
¿Hay azucar en mi cafe?	*ah-ee ah-thoo-cahr ain mee kah-fai*	Is there any sugar in my coffee?
Hay algunos ingléses en el hotel	*ah-ee ahl-goon-ohs een-glais-ais ain ail oh-tail*	There are some English people in the hotel
Hay algunas rocas peligrosas por allí	*ah-ee ahl-goo-nahs roh-kahs pail-ee-groh-sahs pohr ah-Lee*	There are some dangerous rocks over there

Note that usually Some/Any is not translated into Spanish, unless special emphasis is needed when the word **alguno/a** can be used.

Negative formed with **'no'**.

No hay pescado	*noh ah-ee pais-kah-doh*	There isn't any fish
No hay sitio	*noh ah-ee see-tee-oh*	There isn't any room

Much/Little/Many/Few

Él bebe mucha cerveza	*ail bai-bai moo-tshah thair-vai-thah*	He drinks a lot of (much) beer
Tengo poco dinero	*tain-goh poh-koh dee-nai-roh*	I have little money. I have not much money
Hay muchos bancos en la ciudad	*ah-ee moo-tshohs bahn-kohs ain lah thee-oo-dahd*	There are many banks in the town
Él ha bebido pocas copas de vino	*ailah bai-bee-doh poh-kahs koh-pahs dai vee-noh*	He has drunk few glasses of wine. He hasn't drunk many glasses of wine

Remember to use the feminine form if needed – **mucha/poca muchas/pocas**

How much?
How many? – see grammar p 45

More/No More

Más de cien pesetas	*mahs dai thee-ain pai-sai-tahs*	More than a hundred pesetas
Más pan por favor	*mahs pahn pohr fah-vohr*	More bread, please
¿Hay más?	*ahee mahs*	Is there any more?
Un poco más por favor	*oon pohkoh mahs pohr fahvohr*	A little more please
Mucho más	*moo-tshoh mahs*	Much more
Otra vez	*oh-trah vaith*	Once more. Another time
Nunca más	*noon-kah mahs*	Never again
No quiero más sopa, gracias	*noon-kee-ai-roh mahs soh-pah grah-thee-ahs*	No more soup thank you. I don't want any more soup, thank you
No tengo más	*noh tain-goh mahs*	I have no more
No hay más	*noh ahee mahs*	There is no more. There isn't any more

Here/There and Everywhere

¡Venga aquí!	*vehn-gah ah-kee*	Come here!
¡Quédese aquí!	*kai-dai-sai ah-kee*	Stay here!
Es aquí	*ais ahkee*	It's here. Here it is
No es aquí	*noh ais ahkee*	It isn't here
Él no está	*ail noh aistah*	He isn't here
¡Ya viene!	*yah vee-ai-nai*	Here he comes! (lit. already he comes)
Estoy aquí	*ais-tohee ah-kee*	I'm here. Here I am
¿Aquí o allí?	*ahkee oh ah-lee*	Here or there?
¡Por allí!	*pohr ah-lee*	Over there!
¡Hay turismo en todos sitios!	*ahee too-rees-moh aln tohdohs see-tee-ohs*	There are tourists everywhere!
¡Se habla Inglés por todas partes!	*sai ah-blah een-glais pohr toh-dahs pahr-tais*	English is spoken everywhere

Note: you will sometimes hear **'alla'** instead of **'allí'** – they both mean 'there'.

Notice the two different ways of translating 'everywhere'.

EXCLAMATIONS

¡Cuidado!	*koo-ee-dah-doh*	watch out/look out!
¡No me diga!	*noh mai dee-gah*	you don't say! Well, I never did!
¿Verdad?	*vair-dahd*	Is that so? Really?
¡Oiga!	*oh-ee-gah*	heh listen! heh, you! (calling someone's attention)
¡Qué tontería!	*kai tohn-tai-ree-ah*	what nonsense!
¡Madre mía!	*mah-drai mee-ah*	heavens above! good gracious!
¡Caramba!	*kah-rahm-bah*	oh, blast!

WANTS AND WISHES

Quiero irme	*kee-ai-roh eer-mai*	I want to go/leave
Quiero hacerlo	*kee-ai-roh ah-thair-loh*	I want to do it
Quiero fumar	*kee-ai-roh foo-mahr*	I want to smoke
¿Me hace el favor?	*mai ah-thai ail fah-vohr*	Would you be so kind as to . . . ?
¿Qué quiere?	*kai kee-ai-rai*	What do you want?
¿Qué desea usted?	*kai dai-sai-ah oos-taid*	What would you like?
¿Tiene la bondad . . .?	*tee-ai-nai lah bohn-dahd*	Would you be kind enough . . . ?
¿Me puede ayudar?	*mai poo-ai-dai ah-yoo-dahr*	Could you help me?

LIKES AND DISLIKES

¿le gusta Barcelona?	*lai goos-tah bahr-thai-loh-nah*	do you like Barcelona?
no, prefiero Madrid	*noh prai-fee-ai-roh mah-dreed*	no, I prefer Madrid
¿le gusta España?	*lai goos-tah ais-pah-Nah*	do you like Spain?
¿le gusta el vino tinto?	*lai goos-tah ail vee-noh teen-toh*	do you like red wine?
me gusta mucho	*mai goos-tah moo-tshoh*	I like it very much
me gustan mucho	*mai goos-tahn moo-tshoh*	I like them very much
mejor que . . .	*mai-Gohr kai*	better than . . . .
pero prefiero	*pai-roh prai-fee-ai-roh*	but I prefer . . .
y me gusta lo mejor . .	*ee mai goos-tah loh mai-Gohr*	and I like . . . . . best

no me gusta	*noh mai goos-tah*	I don't like (it)
lo detesto	*loh dai-tais-toh*	I hate it
es feo	*ais fai-oh*	it's ugly

PERMISSION AND NECESSITY

¿se puede?	*sai poo-ai-dai*	can/may I?
sí, lo puede coger	*see, loh poo-ai-dai koh-Gair*	yes, you can take it
sí, puede pasar	*see, poo-ai-dai pah-sahr*	yes, you can enter/come through/pass
sí, puede hacerlo	*see, poo-ai-dai ah-thair-loh*	yes, you can do it
no puedo	*noh poo-ai-doh*	I can't
¿se permite?	*sai-pair-mee-tai*	is it allowed?
¿es necesario?	*ais nai-thai-sah-ree-oh*	is it necessary?
¿es voluntario u obligatorio?	*ais voh-loon-tah-ree-oh oo oh-blee-gah-toh-ree-oh*	is it voluntary compulsory?

Note: 'or' = 'o', except when the last letter of the word and the first letter of the next word is also 'o' – then 'or' = 'u'.

¿es facultivo?	*ais fah-kool-tee-voh*	is it optional?

ENQUIRY AND INFORMATION

¿dónde se puede encontrar?	*dohn-dai sai poo-ai-dai ain-kohn-trahr*	where can one find?
¿sabe usted si . . .?	*sah-bai oos-taid see*	do you know if . . .?
¿cómo se llama esta calle?	*koh-moh sai Lah-mah ais-tah kah-Lai*	what is the name of this street?
¿qué pasó?	*kai pah-soh*	what happened?
quiero preguntar por . . .	*kee-ai-roh prai-goon-tahr pohr*	I want to inquire about/for/after . . . .
me gustaría enterarme de	*mai goos-tah-ree-ah ain-tai-rahr-mai-dai*	I should like to know about . . . .
¿puede usted informarme sobre . . .?	*poo-ai-dai oostaid een-fohr-mahr-mai soh-brai*	can you inform me about . . . .
la oficina de turismo	*lah oh-fee-thee-nah dai too-rees-moh*	tourist office
la oficina de informaciones	*lah ohfee-thee-nah dai een-fohr-mah-thee-ohn-ais*	information office

MEETING PEOPLE

Quiero presentarle a usted . . .	*kee-ai-roh prai-sain tahr-lai ah oostaid*	I would like to present . . . to you
Puede usted presentarme a la señora/señor	*poo-ai-dai oostaid prai-sain-tahr-mai ah lah sai-Noh-rah/sai-Nohr*	Would you introduce me to . . . the lady/gentleman . . .
Encantado de conocerle	*ain-Kahn-tah-doh daik oh-noh-thair-lai*	Delighted to meet you
¿A qué hora está en casa?	*ah kai ohrah ais-tah ain kahsah*	At what time are you at home?
Me gustaría ver a . . .	*mai goos-tah-ree-ah vairah*	I should like to see . . .
¿A qué hora vuelve?	*ah kai ohrah voo-ail-vai*	When will he be back?
Pase, por favor	*pah-sai pohr fahvohr*	Do come in please
¿Puede usted esperar unos momentos?	*poo-ai-dai oostaid ais-pai-rahr oonoks mo-main-tohs*	Can you wait a few moments?

No tardará mucho	*noh tahr-dah-rah moo-tshoh*	He will not be very long
Estoy un poco tarde	*ais-tohee oon poh-koh tahr-dai*	I am a little late
¡De nada!	*dai nah-dah*	Not at all!
Siéntese por favor	*see-ain-tai-sai pohr fah-vohr*	Sit down please
Es usted muy amable	*ais oostaid mooee ah-mah-blai*	You are very kind
Recuerdos a . . .	*rai-koo-air-dohs ah*	King regards to . . . .
¿Comó está usted?	*koh-moh ais-tah oostaid*	How are you?
¿Qué tal está usted?	*kai tahl ais-tah oostaid*	How are you? (less formal)
¿Cómo está su padre?	*koh-moh ais-tah soo pah-drai*	How is your father?
¡Me alegro!	*mai ah-lai-groh*	I am very pleased (to hear it)
¡Lo siento!	*loh see-ain-toh*	I am very sorry (to hear it)
¡Que buena noticia!	*kai boo-ai-nah noh-tee-thee-ah*	What good news!

SPEAKING AND UNDERSTANDING

¿Habla usted inglés?	*ahblah oostaid een-glais*	Do you speak English?
Un poco solamente	*oon poh-koh soh-lah-main-tai*	Only a little
¿Hay alguien por aquí que hable inglés?	*ahee ahl-gee-ain pohr ahkee kai ahblai een-glais*	Is there anyone here who speaks English?
¿Entiende? (or) **¿Comprende usted?**	*ain-tee-ain-dai* *kohm-prain-dai oostaid*	Do you understand?
Entiendo si usted habla despacio	*ain-tee-ain-doh see oostaid ahblah dais-pah-theeoh*	I understand if you speak slowly
No comprendo	*noh kohm-prain-doh*	I don't understand
No hable tan deprisa	*noh ahblai tahn dai-pree-sah*	Don't speak so quickly

¿Cómo es .... en inglés?	*koh-moh ais . . . ain een-glais*	How do you say . . . in English? What is . . . in English?
¿Qué significa .....?	*kai seeg-nee-fee-kah*	What does . . . mean?
¿Puede usted repetirlo?	*poo-ai-dai oostaid rai-pai-teer-loh*	Can you repeat it?

PRONOUNS AND POSSESSIVES

Me, You, Him, Her, It, Them

él espera por mí	*ail ais-pai-rah pohr mee*	he is waiting for me
él no espera por mí	*ail noh ais-pai-rah pohr mee*	he is not waiting for me
le conozco	*lai koh-nohth-koh*	I know you/him
no le conozco	*noh lai koh-nohth-koh*	I don't know you/him
¿le conoce usted?	*lai koh-noh-thai oos-taid*	do you know him?
le quiero	*lai kee-ai-roh*	I love/want him/you
la quiero	*lah kee-ai-roh*	I love/want her/it (fem)
lo quiero	*loh kee-ai-roh*	I love/want it (masc)
te quiero	*tai kee-ai-roh*	I love/want you (familiar)
él no me quiere	*ail noh mai kee-ai-rai*	he does not love/want me

lo como siempre	*loh koh-moh see-aim-prai*	I always eat it
aquí está la copa	*ah-kee ais-tah lah koh-pah*	here is the cup
¡tómela!	*toh-mai-lah*	take it (fem)!
¡tómelo!	*toh-mai-loh*	take it (masc)!
aquí están los libros	*ah-kee ais-tahn lohs lee-brohs*	here are the books
¡tómelos!	*toh-mai-lohs*	take them (masc)!
¡no la tome!	*noh lah toh-mai*	don't take it (fem)!
¡beba el vino!	*bai-bah ail vee-noh*	drink the wine!
¡bébalo!	*bai-bah-loh*	drink it (masc)!
¡no beba la cerveza!	*noh bai-bah lah thair-vai-thah*	don't drink the beer!
¡no la beba!	*noh lah bai-bah*	don't drink it (fem)!
¿dónde están las chicas?	*dohn-dai ais-tahn lahs tshee-kahs*	where are the girls?
¡llámelas!	*Lah-mai-lahs*	call them (fem)!

Note that 'le' means 'him' and 'you'. To avoid confusion one can say –

le conozco a él	*lai koh-nohth-koh ah ail*	I know him
le conozco a usted	*lai koh-nohth-koh ah oos-taid*	I know you

When using the imperative the object pronoun joins the end of the verb making one word. This does not occur in the negative. (See also COMMANDS AND REQUESTS).

¡cómalo!	*koh-mah-loh*	eat it!
¡no lo coma!	*noh loh koh-mah*	don't eat it!

To Him/To Her/To Them

¡dígale!	*dee-gah-lai*	tell him/her!
¡dígales!	*dee-gah-lais*	tell them!
¡escríbales!	*ais-kree-bah-lais*	write to them!
¡hábleles!	*ah-blai-lais*	talk to them!
¡pregunte!	*prai-goon-tai*	ask!
¡conteste!	*kohn-tais-tai*	answer!
¡no les hable!	*noh lais ah-blai*	don't speak to them!

¡preguntémosle!	*prai-goon-tai-mohs-lai*	let's ask him/her!
¡no les escriba!	*noh lais ais-kree-bah*	don't write to them!
¡escríbales hoy!	*ais-kree-bah-lais oh-ee*	write to them today!
¡le hablan!	*lai ah-blahn*	they are speaking to him/her/you!
¡les escribimos!	*lais ais-kree-bee-mohs*	we are writing to them!

Of The/To The

La mujer del profesor	*lah moo-Gair dail proh-fai-sohr*	The teacher's wife
La casa de mi padre	*lah kah-sah dai mee pah-drai*	My father's house
La maleta de la señora	*lah mah-lai-tah dai lah sai-Noh-rah*	The lady's case
Los padres de los niños	*lohs pah-drais dai lohs nee-Nohs*	The parents of the children
El coche del amigo de mi hermana	*ail koh-tshai dail ah-mee-goh dai mee air-mah-nah*	My sister's friend's car

El nombre del hotel	*ail nohm-brai dail oh-tail*	The name of the hotel
Mándelo al señor	*mahn-dai-loh ahl saiNohr*	Send it to the gentle-man
Hable con la señora	*ah-blai kohn lahsai-Noh-rah*	Speak to the lady (Lit. speak WITH the lady)
Voy a la estación	*vohee ah lah ais-tah thee-ohn*	I am going to the station

Note that the 's, meaning possession in English, does not exist in Spanish. We have to use 'of the' instead (the man's glass – the glass of the man).

When 'of the' and 'to the' are followed by a masculine singular noun, remember these contractions:

del instead of '**de el**'
al instead of '**a el**'

This That These Those

este libro es muy interesante	*ais-tai lee-broh ais moo-ee een-tai-rai-sahn-tai*	this book is very interesting
esta carta es para usted	*ais-tah kahr-tah ais pah-rah oos-taid*	this letter is for you

esto es una tontería	*ais-toh ais oon-ah tohn-tai-ree-ah*	this is ridiculous
prefiero estos pantalones	*prai-fee-ai-roh ais-tohs pahn-tah-loh-nais*	I prefer these trousers
estos sobres están rotos	*ais-tohs soh-brais ais-tahn roh-tohs*	these envelopes are torn
me gusta ese disco	*mai goos-tah ai-sai dees-koh*	I like that record
no me apetece aquel chico	*noh mai ah-pai-tai-thai ah-kail tshee-koh*	I don't fancy that boy (over there)
esa playa es muy limpia	*ai-sah plah-yah ais moo-ee leem-pee-ah*	that beach is very clean
eso, me enfadó	*ais-oh mai ain-fah-doh*	that made me cross
esos hoteles son muy caros	*ai-sohs oh-tai-lais sohn moo-ee kah-rohs*	those hotels are very expensive
¡mire aquellos barcos!	*mee-rai ah-kai-Lohs bahr-kohs*	look at those boats (over there)!
¿le gustaría esas camisas?	*lai goos-tah-ree-ah ai-sahs kah-mee-sahs*	would you like those shirts?

Note: (1) The two forms of 'that' in Spanish:

¿cuál quiere, ese coche o aquél?	*koo-ahl kee-ai-rai, aisai koh-tshai oh ah-kail*	which do you want, that car (nearby) or that one (over there)?

(2) **eso** and **esto** – the neuter forms – are only used to express general feelings or a summary of an idea. NEVER a definite noun.

esto es bueno	*ais-toh ais boo-ai-noh*	this is good/allright
eso no vale la pena	*ai-soh noh vah-lai lah pai-nah*	that's not worth the trouble

My Your His Her etc

Mi hermano	*mee air-mah-noh*	My brother
Mi hermana	*mee air-mah-nah*	My sister
Mis padres	*mees pah-drais*	My parents
Su padre	*soo pah-drai*	His father
Su madre	*soo mah-drai*	His mother
Sus niños	*soos nee-Nohs*	His children
Su tía	*soo tee-ah*	Your aunt

Sus cigarrillos	*soos thee-gah-rree-Lohs*	Your cigarettes
Nuestro jardín	*noo-ais-troh Gahr-deen*	Our garden
Nuestros niños	*noo-ais-trohs nee-Nohs*	Our children
Sus primos	*soos pree-mohs*	Their cousins
Nuestra casa	*noo-ais-trah kah-sah*	Our house

Unlike all other adjectives in Spanish which agree in gender with their noun, my, his, her, your, excepting **'nuestro, nuestra'** (our,) do not. They do however agree in number, by adding an 's'.

Su gato	*soo gah-toh*	His/her/your cat
Sus gatos	*soos gah-tohs*	His/her/your cats
Mine Yours His Hers etc.		
este es mío	*ais-tai ais me-oh*	this (masc) is mine
estas son mías	*ais-tahs sohn mee-ahs*	these (fem) are mine
ése es suyo	*ai-sai ais soo-yoh*	that (masc) is yours/his/hers
esa mesa es suya	*ai-sah mai-sah ais soo-yah*	that (fem) table is yours/his/hers

quiero el suyo	*kee-ai-roh ail soo-yoh*	I want yours/his/hers (masc)
me gusta la suya	*mai goos-tah lah soo-yah*	I like yours/his/hers/ (fem)
ésos son nuestros	*ais-ohs sohn noo-ais-trohs*	those (masc) are ours
éstas son suyas	*ais-tahs sohn soo-yahs*	these (fem) are theirs/ yours
mi casa y la suya	*mee kah-sah ee lah soo-yah*	my house and yours/ his/hers
coma lo suyo no lo mío	*koh-mah loh soo-yoh noh loh mee-oh*	eat yours/theirs not mine (sing)
me gusta la nuestra más que la suya	*mai goos-tah lah noo-ais-trah mahs kai lah soo-yah*	I like ours (fem) better than yours/ his/hers (fem)

Note: that all these possessive pronouns are preceeded by **el, la, los, las** (the) except when the verb **'ser'** (to be) is used,

Myself Yourself
Himself etc.

lo haré yo mismo	*loh ah-rai yoh mees-moh*	I shall do it myself (masc)

¿va a hacerlo usted misma?	*vah ah ah-thair-loh oos-taid mees-mah*	are you going to do it yourself (fem)?
lo comerá él mismo	*loh koh-mai-rah ail mees-moh*	he will eat it himself
lo hará ella misma	*loh ah-rah ai-Lah mees-mah*	she will do it herself
quieren hacerlo ellos (ellas) mismos (as)	*kee-ai-rain ah-thair-loh ai-Lohs (ai-Lahs) mees-mohs (ahs)*	they want to do it themselves

Note: that **yo mismo, usted mismo,** etc., is used only for greater emphasis. Myself, yourself, himself etc. are also translated by the reflexive verbs in Spanish, e.g.:

lavarse	*la vahr-sai*	to wash oneself
me lavo	*mai lah-voh*	I wash myself
nos lavamos	*nohs lah-vah-mohs*	we wash ourselves

'TO BE' AND 'TO GO'

¿es inglés, verdad?	*ais een-glais, vair-dahd*	you/he are English, aren't you?
¿la niña es muy bonita, verdad?	*lah nee-Nah ais moo-ee boh-nee-tah, vair-dahd*	the little girl is very pretty, isn't she?
¿habla usted español, verdad?	*ah-blah oos-taid ais-pah-Nohl, vair-dahd*	you speak Spanish, don't you?

The simplest and most widely used translation of all the English 'question tags' like isn't, aren't you etc. . . . is **¿verdad?**' (lit. 'true?') or **'no es verdad'** (lit. 'is it not true?').

I Am Going To .....

voy a salir	*voh-ee ah sah-leer*	I am going to go out
voy a comer	*voh-ee ah koh-mair*	I am going to eat
¿va usted a bañarse?	*vah oos-taid ah bah-Nahr-sai*	are you going to swim?

ella va a comprar unos zapatos	*ai-Lah vah ah kohm-prahr oo-nohs thah-pah-tohs*	she is going to buy some shoes
¿vamos a salir, o no?	*vah-mohs ah sah-leer oh noh*	are we going to go out or not?
¿van a tocar la gui-tarra?	*vahn ah toh-kahr lah gee-tah-rrah*	are they going to play the guitar?

Note: As in English the immediate future (I am going to . . .) is translated by the verb **'IR'** (to go), **yo voy, usted va**, etc., but must be followed by the preposition **'a'** (to).

The more distant future, is translated by special endings to the actual verb, and not by additional words such as 'will' and 'shall'.

'It Is . . . . .' 'It Was . . . . .'

1) está bien	*ais-tah bee-ain*	it's good
estaba bien	*ais-tah-bah bee-ain*	it was good
fué fácil	*foo-ai fah-theel*	it was easy
fué difícil	*foo-ai dee-fee-theel*	it was difficult
es verdad	*ais vair-dahd*	it's true
¿era verdad?	*ai-rah vair-dahd*	was it true?

mire el vaso, está roto	*mee-rai ail vah-soh, ais-tah roh-toh*	look at the glass, it's broken
no coma la carne, está mala	*noh koh-mah lah kahr-nai, ais-tah mah-lah*	don't eat the meat, it's bad

Note: that 'it' is NOT translated.

(2) It is = **son las . . .**
It was **eran las . . .** when speaking of time

son las seis	*sohn lahs sai-ees*	it's six o'clock
son las diez	*sohn lahs dee-aith*	it's ten o'clock
eran las tres	*ai-rahn lahs trais*	it was three o'clock
BUT: **es la una**	*ais lah oonah*	it's one o'clock
era la una	*ai-rah lah oonah*	it was one o'clock

(3) It is . . . **hace . . .**
It was . . . **hacía . . .** when speaking of weather

hace buen tiempo	*ah-thai boo-ain tee-aim-poh*	it's fine
hace sol	*ah-thai sohl*	it's sunny
hacía frío	*ah-thee-ah free-oh*	it was cold

NUMBERS

0	cero	*thai-roh*
1	uno	*oon-oh*
2	dos	*dohs*
3	tres	*trais*
4	cuatro	*koo-ah-troh*
5	cinco	*theen-koh*
6	seis	*sai-ees*
7	siete	*see-ai-tai*
8	ocho	*oh-tshoh*
9	nueve	*noo-ai-vai*
10	diez	*dee-aith*
11	once	*ohn-thai*
12	doce	*doh-thai*
13	trece	*trai-thai*
14	catorce	*kah-tohr-thai*
15	quince	*keen-thai*

16	**diez y seis**	*dee-aith ee sai-ees*
17	**diez y siete**	*dee-aith ee see-ai-tai*
18	**diez y ocho**	*dee-aith ee oh-tshoh*
19	**diez y nueve**	*dee-aith ee noo-ai-vai*
20	**veinte**	*vai-een-tai*
21	**veinte y uno**	*vai-een-tai ee oo-noh*
22	**veinte y dos**	*vai-een-tai ee dohs*
23	**veinte y tres**	*vai-een-tai ee trais*
30	**treinta**	*trai-een-tah*
31	**treinta y uno**	*trai-een-tah ee oon-oh*
40	**cuarenta**	*koo-ah-rain-tah*
50	**cincuenta**	*theen-koo-ain-tah*
60	**sesenta**	*sai-sain-tah*
70	**setenta**	*sai-tain-tah*
80	**ochenta**	*oh-tshain-tah*
90	**noventa**	*noh-vain-tah*
100	**cien**	*thee-ain*
101	**ciento uno**	*thee-ain-toh oon-oh*
200	**dos cientos**	*dohs thee-ain-tohs*
1,000	**mil**	*meel*
2,000	**dos mil**	*dohs meel*

100,000	**cien mil**	*thee-ain meel*
1,000,000	**un millón**	*oon mee-Lohn*
2,000,000	**dos millones**	*dohs mee-Lohnais*
1973	**mil nueve cientos setenta y tres**	*meel nooaivai thee-ain-tohs sai-taintah ee trais*
1st	**primero**	*pree-mairoh*
2nd	**segundo**	*sai-goondoh*
3rd	**tercero**	*tair-thairoh*
4th	**cuarto**	*koo-ahr-toh*
5th	**quinto**	*keen-toh*
6th	**sexto**	*saix-toh*
7th	**séptimo**	*saipteemoh*
8th	**octavo**	*ohk-tah-voh*
9th	**noveno**	*noh-vainoh*
10th	**décimo**	*dai-thee-moh*

Note: The first of the month is **el primero de . . .** but the second, third, fourth etc., is **el dos, el tres, el cuatro de . . .**

WEIGHTS AND MEASURES

Un kilo = 1,000 gramos =	*oon kee-loh = meel grahmohs*	2.2lb
Un medio kilo = 500 gramos =	*.oon maideeoh keeloh = kee-neeain-tohs grahmohs*	1.1lb (half a kilogram)

1 ounce = 28 grammes, 1 pound = 453 grammes, 1 cwt = 50·8 kilograms

Pesado	*pai-sah-doh*	heavy (also can mean 'boring')
Ligero	*lee-Gai-roh*	light
Pesar	*paisahr*	to weigh
El peso	*ail paisoh*	the weight
La balanza	*lah bah-lahnthah*	the scales

1 metro=100 centímetros=1.000 milímetros=39 inches – *oon maitroh= thee-ain thaintee-maitrohs=meel meelee-maitrohs*

1 centímetro=10 milímetros=2/5 of an inch – *oon thain-tee-maitroh= dee-aith mee-lee-mai-trohs*

1 kilometro=1,000 metros=5/8 of a mile – *oon kee-loh-mai troh=meel maitrohs*

1 inch=**2½ centimetros**	1 foot=**30 centímetros**
1 yard=**90 centimetros**	5 miles=**8 kilometros**

Largo (corto)	*lahrgoh (cohrtoh)*	long (short)
Grande (pequeño)	*grahn-dai (pai-kai-Noh)*	big (little, small)
Ancho (estrecho)	*ahn-tshoh (ais-trai-tshoh)*	wide (narrow)
Alto (bajo)	*ahltoh (bahGoh)*	high (low)
Profundo (poco profundo)	*proh-foon-doh (pohkoh)*	deep (shallow)
Cinco metros de largo	*theenkoh maitrohs dai lahr-goh*	5 metres long
Tres metros de largo dor dos de ancho	*trais maitrohs dai lahrgoh pohr dohs dai ahntshoh*	3 metres long by two metres wide

1 litro – *leetroh*	= $1\frac{3}{4}$ pints	1 pint = $\frac{1}{2}$ litro
2 litros	= $3\frac{1}{2}$ pints	1 quart = 1 litro
5 litros	= 1 gallon $\frac{3}{4}$ pints	1 gallon = $4\frac{1}{2}$ litros

Note: All these equivalents are approximate.

NOTICES

Entrada	entrance
Salida	exit
Abierto	open
Cerrado	closed
Prohibido fumar	smoking prohibited
Prohibido bañarse	bathing forbidden
Prohibido hablar con el conductor	it is forbidden to talk to the driver
Empujar	push
Tirar	pull
Cerrar	close
Servicios	toilets
Señoras	ladies
Señores	gents
Caballeros	gents
Ocupado	occupied
Libre	free

Caliente	hot
Frío	cold
Entrada prohibida	entrance forbidden to public
Parada	bus, taxi stop
Para alquilar	for hire
Para vender	for sale
Entre sin llamar	enter without knocking
Pase sin llamar	enter without knocking
Alarma	alarm
Prohibido escupir	spitting forbidden
Recién pintado	fresh paint
Prohibido el paso	no thoroughfare
Se prohibe fijar carteles	billposting prohibited
Prohibido asomarse por la ventana	forbidden to lean out of the window
Prohibido pisar la hierba	do not walk on the grass

EATING OUT

Remember that mealtimes in Spain are quite different from England. Lunch is generally sometime after 2 p.m. – this is the heaviest meal of the day and usually consists of three courses. Anytime between 5 p.m. and 7 p.m. is 'teatime' – though not as we know it. This will consist of a beer, wine or coffee to drink, with an omelette, ham and cheese roll, and perhaps some sweet bun. Dinner follows at about 9.30 p.m. onwards, and is a smaller version of lunch. Despite the difference the Spanish, particularly in the heavy tourist areas, are very accommodating and there is rarely a moment during the day when you cannot get a meal.

A few words about the 'Bars'. In their popularity, quantity and purpose, they are a mixture of our pubs and coffee bars. Closed for only a few hours during the night, there is no drink, alcoholic or otherwise that cannot be bought! There is always a variety of **'tapas'** or **'pinchos'** (see below) to choose from, and some bars automatically serve you a few olives or pieces of fish with your glass of wine. No restrictions to children are enforced. Finally it's as well to remember that every restaurant by law SHOULD produce a **'menú turistico'**. This three course all inclusive menu (which will vary enormously in quality, though not much in variety – depending on the restaurant) costs from 60 pesetas.

TIPPING

Food and Drink. Don't make the mistake of overtipping. Meals, 10 per cent unless service is included (**servicio incluido**). In the bars, a 1 peseta tip on a glass of wine or coffee is usual. Stick to the 10 per cent if you have a snack as well.

Taxis. Usual to tip about 7 per cent. Suitcases that you can't pass over as hand luggage, are charged extra.

pinchos y tapas	*peen-tsohs ee tah-pahs*	snacks at the bar
aceitunas	*ah-thai-ee-too-nahs*	olives
anchoas	*ahn-tshoh-ahs*	anchovies
atún	*ah-toon*	tuna fish
angulas	*ahn-goo-lahs*	elvers (baby eels)
boquerones	*boh-kai-rohn-ais*	unsalted anchovies
bonito	*boh-nee-toh*	fish similar to tuna fish

berberechos	*bair-bai-rai-tshohs*	winkles
chorizo	*tshoh-ree-thoh*	spicy pork sausage with red peppers
calamares	*kah-lah-mah-rais*	squid
caracoles	*kah-rah-koh-lais*	snails
chanquetes	*tshahn-kai-tais*	fried whitebait
caviar	*kah-vee-ahr*	caviar
cigalas	*thee-gah-lahs*	a large shrimp
ensaladilla rusa	*ain-sah-lah-dee-Lah roo-sah*	Russian salad
gambas	*gahm-bahs*	shrimps
huevo duro	*oo-ai-voh doo-roh*	hard boiled egg
jamón serrano	*Gah-mohn sai-rrah-noh*	smoked ham
jamón york	*Gah-mohn yohrk*	ham
langostinos	*lahn-gohs-tee-nohs*	prawns
langosta	*lahn-gohs-tah*	lobster
ostras	*ohs-trahs*	oysters
pulpo	*pool-poh*	octopus
pimienta picante	*pee-mee-ain-tah pee-kahn-tai*	hot peppers

patatas fritas	*pah-tah-tahs free-tahs*	crisps or chips
patatas bravas	*pah-tah-tahs brah-vahs*	fried potato chunks with a spicy sauce
pepinillos	*pai-pee-nee-Lohs*	gherkins
sardina	*sahr-dee-nah*	sardine
tortilla	*tohr-tee-Lah*	omellete (always made with potato and onion in bars)
toreras	*toh-rai-rahs*	a small skewer of pickled vegetables
queso	*kai-soh*	cheese
quisquillas	*kees-kee-Lahs*	tiny shrimps

SPANISH MENUS

aceite	*ah-thai-ee-tai*	oil
aceitunas	*ah-thai-ee-too-nahs*	olives
acelgas	*ah-thail-gahs*	green vegetable similar to spinach
ajo	*ah-Goh*	garlic
albaricoque	*ahl-bah-ree-koh-kai*	apricots
albóndigas	*ahl-bohn-dee-gahs*	meat balls
alcachofa	*ahl-kah-tshoh-fah*	artichoke
almejas	*ahl-mai-Gahs*	clams
almendras	*ahl-main-drahs*	almonds
anchoas	*ahn-tshoh-ahs*	anchovies
anguila	*ahn-gee-lah*	eel
angula	*ahn-goo-lah*	elver
ápio	*ah-pee-oh*	celery
arenque	*ah-rain-kai*	herring
arroz	*ah-rrohth*	rice

arroz a la cubana	*ah-rrohth ah lah koo-bah-nah*	with a fried egg and tomato sauce
arroz con leche	*ah-rrohthkohn lait-shai*	rice pudding
atún	*ah-toon*	tuna fish
azucar	*ah-thoo-kahr*	sugar
baba al ron	*bah-bah alh rohn*	rum baba
bacalao	*bah-kah-lah-oh*	cod
berenjenas	*bai-rain-Gai-nahs*	aubergine
besamel	*bai-sah-mail*	white sauce
besugo	*bai-soo-goh*	bream
boquerones	*boh-kai-roh-nais*	unsalted anchovies
butifarra	*boo-tee-fah-rrah*	large pork sausage – typical in Cataluña
caballa	*kah-bah-Lah*	mackerel
calabacín	*kah-lah-bah-theen*	small pumpkin
calamares	*kah-lah-mah-rais*	squids
calamares en su tinta	*ain soo teen-tah*	in ink
caldo	*kahl-doh*	thin soup
canela	*kah-nai-lah*	cinnamon
canelones	*kah-nai-loh-nais*	pasta filled with meat
cangrejo	*kahn-grai-Goh*	crab

capón	*kah-pohn*	capon
caracoles	*kah-rah-koh-lais*	snails
caramelo	*kah-rah-mail-o*	burnt sugar sauce
cebolla	*thai-boh-Lah*	onion
cerdo	*thair-doh*	pork
cerezas	*thai-rai-thahs*	cherries
champiñón	*tshahm-pee-Nohn*	small mushrooms
chatoubrian	*tshah-toh-oo-bree-ahn*	grilled steak
chocolate	*tshoh-koh-lah-tai*	chocolate
churrasco	*tshoo-rrahs-koh*	thick barbecue steak
churros	*tshoo-rohs*	finger sized strips of fried pancake batter – very typical dipped in hot chocolate
ciruela	*thee-roo-ai-lah*	plum
claudia	*clah-oo-dee-ah*	greengage
cocido	*koh-thee-doh*	vegetable and ham based stew
col	*kohl*	cabbage

coles de Bruselas	*koh-lais dai Broo-sai-lahs*	Brussel sprouts
coliflor	*koh-lee-flohr*	cauliflower
conejo	*koh-nai-Goh*	rabbit
congrio	*kohn-gree-oh*	conger eel
corazón	*koh-rah-thohn*	heart
cordero	*kohr-dai-roh*	lamb
codorniz	*koh-dohr-neeth*	quail
croqueta	*kroh-kai-tah*	croquette
ensalada	*ain-sah-lah-dah*	tomato and lettuce salad
ensaladilla rusa	*ain-sah-lah-dee-Lah roo-sah*	Russian salad
entremeses de fiambres	*ain-trai-mai-sais dai fee-ahm-brais*	plate of assorted smoked meats
escabeche	*ais-kah-bai-tshai*	pickled white fish
espaguetis	*ais-pah gai-tees*	spaghetti
espárragos	*ais-pah-rrah-gohs*	asparagus
espinacas	*ais-pee-nah-kahs*	spinach

estofado	*ais-toh-fah-doh*	rich meat and potato based stew
fabada	*fah-bah-dah*	pork and butter bean stew
faisán	*fah-ee-sahn*	pheasant
frambuesa	*frahm-boo-ai-sah*	raspberry
fresa	*frai-sah*	strawberry
fresón	*frai-sohn*	large strawberry
fideos	*fee-dai-ohs*	vermicelli
flán	*flahn*	cream caramel
galleta	*gah-Lai-tah*	sweet biscuit
gallina	*gah-Lee-nah*	hen
gallo	*gah-Loh*	cock
gambas	*gahm-bahs*	shrimps
garbanzos	*gahr-bahn-thohs*	chick peas
gazpacho	*gahth-pah-tshoh*	cold soup of onion, peppers, tomato, cucumber and seasoning
guisantes	*gee-sahn-tais*	peas
habas	*ah-bahs*	broad beans

harina	*ah-ree-nah*	flour
helado	*ai-lah-doh*	ice cream
hielo	*ee-ai-loh*	ice
higado	*ee-gah-doh*	liver
huevos	*oo-ai-vohs*	eggs
huevos al plato	*ahl plah-to*	a plate of eggs
huevos escaldados	*ais-kahl-dah-dohs*	poached
huevos fritos	*free-tohs*	fried
huevos pasados por agua	*pah-sah-dohs pohr. ah-goo-ah*	boiled
huevos revueltos	*rai-voo-ail-tohs*	scrambled
jamón	*Gah-mohn*	ham
jamón serrano	*sai-rrah-noh*	smoked
jamón york	*yohrk*	sweet ham
jeréz	*Gai-raith*	sherry
judías blancas	*Goo-dee-ahs blahn-kahs*	butter beans
judías verdes	*vair-dais*	green beans
judías pintas	*peen-tahs*	a mixture of red and butter beans

langosta	*lahn-gohs-tah*	lobster
langostinos	*lahn-gohs-tee-nohs*	prawns
leche	*lai-tshai*	milk
lechón	*lai-tshohn*	suckling pig
lechuga	*lai-tshoo-gah*	lettuce
legumbres	*lai-goom-brais*	vegetables
lengua	*lain-goo-ah*	tongue
lenguado	*lain-goo-ah-doh*	sole
lentejas	*lain-tai-Gahs*	lentils
liebre	*lee-ai-brai*	hare
limón	*lee-mohn*	lemon
macarrones	*mah-kah-rroh-nais*	maccaroni
manos de cerdo	*mah-nohs dai thair-doh*	pigs trotters
manzana	*mahn-thah-nah*	apple
mejillones	*mai-Gee-Loh-nais*	mussels
melocotón	*mai-loh-koh-tohn*	peach
melón	*mai-lohn*	melon
menudillos	*mai-noo-dee-Lohs*	giblets
merengue	*mai-rain-gai*	meringue
merluza	*mair-loo-thah*	hake

mero	*mai-roh*	brill
miel	*mee-ail*	honey
mostaza	*mos-stah-thah*	mustard
nabo	*nah-boh*	turnip
naranja	*nah-rahn-Gah*	orange
nata	*nah-tah*	cream
tallarines	*tai-ya-reen-es*	noodles
nueces	*noo-ai-thais*	nuts
nuez de nogal	*noo-aith dai noh-gahl*	walnut
paella	*pah-ai-Lah*	typical rice dish with fish or meat – varies in each region
paloma	*pah-loh-mah*	pigeon
pan	*pahn*	bread
paradilla de mariscos	*pah-rah-dee-Lah dai mah-rees-kohs*	plate of grilled shell fish
pasa	*pah-sah*	dried fruit
patatas	*pah-tah-tahs*	potatoes
al horno	*ahl ohr-noh*	roast
cocidas	*koh-thee-dahs*	boiled

fritas	*free-tahs*	fried or chips
puré de patatas	*poo-rai dai pah-tah-tahs*	mashed
pato	*pah-toh*	duck
pato a la naranja	*ah lah nah-rahn-Gah*	with orange
pavo	*pah-voh*	turkey
pera	*pai-rah*	pear
perdíz	*pair-deeth*	partridge
perejíl	*pai-rai-Geel*	parsley
pichón	*pee-tshohn*	small pigeon
pisto	*pees-toh*	stewed vegetables usually, peppers, tomatoes, onions beans etc.
plátano	*plah-tah-noh*	banana
pollo	*poh-Loh*	chicken
puerros	*poo-ai-rrohs*	leeks
pulpo	*pool-poh*	octopus
rábano	*rah-bah-noh*	raddish
rape	*rah-pai*	fish similar to squid or octopus

ravioli	*rah-vee-oh-lee*	ravioli
remolacha	*rai-moh-lah-tshah*	beet
riñones	*ree-Noh-nais*	kidneys
sal	*sahl*	salt
salchichas	*sahl-tshee-tshahs*	sausages
salmón	*sahl-mohn*	salmon
salmonetes	*sahl-moh-nai-tais*	red mullet
sandía	*sahn-dee-ah*	red water melon
sardinas	*sahr-dee-nahs*	sardines
sesos	*sai-sohs*	brains
setas	*sai-tahs*	mushrooms
sopa	*soh-pah*	thin soup, usually with vermicelli
tapioca	*tah-pee-oh-kah*	tapioca
tartitas	*tah-tee-tas*	little tarts
ternera	*tair-nai-rah*	veal
tocino	*toh-thee-noh*	fatty bacon
tomate	*toh-mah-tai*	tomato
tortilla	*tohr-tee-Lah*	omelette
española	*ais-pah-Noh-lah*	with potato and onion
francesa	*frahn-thai-sah*	plain

trucha	*troo-tshah*	trout
uvas	*oo-vahs*	grapes
vaca	*vah-kah*	beef
vainilla	*vah-ee-nee-Lah*	vanilla
vinagre	*vee-nah-grai*	vinegar
yema	*yai-mah*	egg yolk
zanahorias	*thah-nah-oh-ree-ahs*	carrots

The following is a useful list of cooking and general 'terms' that can be found on most menus.

a la parilla	*ah lah pah-ree-Lah*	grilled over charcoal
a la plancha	*ah lah plahn-tshah*	grilled
ajillo	*ah-Gee-Loh*	fried with garlic
al gratín	*ahl grah-teen*	with cheese topping
al horno	*ahl ohr-noh*	baked
asado	*ah-sah-doh*	roast
bocadillo	*boh-kah-dee-Loh*	filled bread roll
buñuelo	*boo-Noo-ai-loh*	fritter
carne	*kahr-nai*	meat
carne picada	*kahr-nai pee-kah-dah*	minced meat
chuleta de . . .	*tshoo-lai-tah dai*	chop

con mayonesa	*kohn mah-yoh-nai-sah*	with mayonaise
con vinagreta	*kohn vee-nah-grai-tah*	with oil and vinegar dressing
de lata	*dai lah-tah*	tinned
empanada	*aimpah-nah-dah*	in pastry
escalope	*ais-kah-loh-pai*	escalope
filete de . . .	*fee-lai-tai dai*	fillet of . . .
fruta	*froo-tah*	fruit
lomo	*loh-moh*	loin
mermelada	*mair-mai-lah-dah*	jam
pechuga de	*pai-tshoo-gah dai*	breast of . . .
pescado	*pais-kah-doh*	fish
rebozada	*rai-boh-thah-dah*	fried with egg and flour coating
relleno	*rai-Lai-noh*	stuffed
salsa picante	*sahl-sah pee-kahn-tai*	spicy sauce
solomillo	*soh-loh-mee-Loh*	sirloin
sandwich	*sahn-dweech*	sandwich

Part II

ASKING ONE'S WAY

Which is the best way to . . . ?	**¿cómo se puede ir a . . . ?**	*koh-moh sai poo-ai-dai eer ah*
which is the best way for . . . ?	**¿por dónde es mejor para . . . ?**	*pohr dohn-dai ais mai-Gohr pah-rahr*
where does this street go . . . ?	**¿a dónde va esta calle?**	*ah dohn-dai vah ais-tah kah-Lai*
Is . . . Street far from here?	**¿está muy lejos la calle . . . ?**	*ais-tah moo-ee lai-Gohs lah kah-Lai*
excuse me where is the bus stop?	**usted perdone, ¿dónde está la parada del autobus?**	*oos-taid pair-doh-nai, dohn-dai ais-tah lah pah-rah-dah dail ah-oo-toh-boos*

Does this bus go to . . . ?	¿Va este autobus por . . . ?	*Vahais-tai ah-oo-toh-boos pohr . . .*
where do I have to get off?	¿dónde tengo que bajar?	*dohn-dai tain-goh kai bah-Gahr*
do I get out here?	¿bajo aquí?	*bah-Goh ah-kee*
Is it far from here?	¿está muy lejos de aquí?	*ais-tah moo-ee lai-Gohs dai ah-kee*
Can I walk there?	¿se puede ir caminando?	*sai poo-ai-dai eer kah-mee-nahn-doh*
more or less 20 mins walk	más o menos veinte minutos caminando	*mahs oh mai-nohs vai-een-tai mee-noo-tohs kah-mee-nahn-doh*
go straight on	siga recto	*see-gah raik-toh*
take the first on the right (left)	tome la primera a la derecha (izquierda)	*toh-mai lah pree-mai-rah ah lah dai-rai-tshah (eeth-kee-air-dah)*
cross the square	cruce la plaza	*kroo-thai lah plah-thah*
on the right	a la derecha	*ah lah dai-rai-tshah*

on the left	**a la izquierda**	*ah lah eeth-kee-air-dah*
on the corner of the street	**en la esquina de la calle**	*ain lah ais-kee-nah dai lah kah-Lai*
underground	**metro**	*mai-troh*
taxi	**taxi**	*tah-xee*
to get in	**subir**	*soo-beer*
to get out	**bajar**	*bah-Gahr*
main road	**carretera principal**	*kah-rrai-tai-rah preen-thee-pahl*
cross roads	**cruces**	*kroo-thais*
fork (in the road)	**una bifurcación**	*bee-foor-kah-thee-ohn*
traffic lights	**semáforos**	*sai-mah-foh-rohs*
sign post	**la señal**	*sai-Nahl*
high street (of a town)	**calle principal**	*kah-Lai preen-thee-pahl*
bends (in a road)	**curvas**	*koor-vahs*

TRAVEL

Travelling	**viajes**	*vee-ah-Gaids*
the journey	**el viaje**	*vee-ah-Gai*
to travel/make a journey	**viajar**	*vee-ah-Gahr*
to go abroad	**ir al extranjero**	*eer ahl ais-trahn-Gai-roh*
to the seaside	**ir al mar**	*eer ahl mahr*
to the mountains	**ir a las montañas**	*eer ah lahs mohn-tah-Nahs*
by train	**en tren**	*eer ain train*
by boat	**en barco**	*eer ain bahr-koh*
by car	**en coche**	*eer ain koh-tshai*
by air	**en avión**	*eer ain ah-vee-ohn*
To go on foot	**ir a pie**	*eer ah peeai*
on a bycicle	**en bicicleta**	*ain bee-thee-Klai-tah*
by land	**por tierra**	*pohr tee-ai-rah*
by sea	**por mar**	*pohr mahr*

journey there	**viaje**	*vee-ah-Gai*
journey back	**la vuelta**	*voo-ail-tah*
break in journey	**un descanso**	*dais-kahn-soh*
a round trip	**un viaje circular**	*vee-ah-Gai theer-koo-lahr*
route	**la ruta**	*roo-tah*
passport (with visa)	**pasaporte (con visa)**	*pah-sah-pohr-tai (Kohn vee-sah)*
travel agency	**agencia de viaje**	*ah-Gain-thee-ah dai vee-ah-Gai*
time table	**el horario**	*oh-rah-ree-oh*
railway time table	**el horario de tren**	*oh-rah-ree-oh dai train*
time of departure	**hora de salida**	*oh-rah dai sah-lee-dah*
time of arrival	**hora de llegada**	*oh-rah dai Lai-gah-dah*
When is the next train/boat/plane to . . . ?	**¿cuándo sale el próximo tren/barco/avión por . .?**	*koo-ahn-doh sah-lai ail proh-xee-moh train/bahr-koh/ah-vee-ohn pohr . . .*
When does it arrive at . . . ?	**¿cuándo llega a . . .?**	*koo-ahn-doh Lai-gah ah . . .*

booking office	**el despacho de billetes**	*dais-pah-tshoh dai bee-Lai-tais*
small window	**la ventanilla**	*vain-tah-nee-Lah*
return ticket	**billete de ida y vuelta**	*bee-Lai-tai dai ee-da ee voo-ail-tah*
reduced price	**precio reducido**	*prai-thee-oh rai-doo-thee-doh*
supplement	**suplemento**	*soo-plai-main-toh*
valid for	**válido para**	*vah-lee-doh pah-rah*
How long is my ticket valid?	**¿mi billete es válido para cuánto tiempo?**	*mee bee-Lai-tai ais vah-lee-doh pah-rah koo-ahn-toh tee-aim-poh*
to book a seat	**reservar un asiento**	*rai-sair-vahr oon ah-see-ain-toh*
corner (window) seat	**al lado de la ventana**	*ah lah-doh dai lah vain-tah-nah*
facing the engine	**mirando hacia delante**	*mee-rahn-doh ah-thee-ah dai-lahn-tai*
with back to engine	**mirando hacia atrás**	*mee-rahn-doh ah-thee-ah ah-trahs*

a berth in the sleeping car	**una litera**	*oon-ah lee-tai-rah*
an upper/lower berth	**litera arriba/abajo**	*lee-tai-rah ah-rree-bah/ah-bah-Goh*
a bed in a private compartment	**una cama**	*oon-ah kah-mah*
THE LUGGAGE	**el equipaje**	*ail ai-kee-pah-Gai*
trunk	**un baúl**	*bah-ool*
suitcase	**una maleta**	*mah-lai-tah*
travelling bag	**un maletín de viaje**	*mah-lai-teen dai vee-ah-Gai*
chest	**un cofre**	*koh-frai*
air cushion	**un cojín de aire**	*koh-Geen dai ah-ee-rai*
rucksack	**una mochila**	*moh-tshee-lah*
basket	**una cesta**	*thais-tah*
hamper	**un canasto**	*kah-nahs-toh*
travelling rug	**una manta**	*mahn-tah*
to pack	**hacer las maletas**	*ah-thair lahs mah-lai-tahs*

to pack something	**poner algo en la maleta**	*poh-nair ahl-goh ain lah mah-lai-tah*
to unpack	**desembalar**	*dais-aim-bah-lahr*
to register one's luggage	**facturar el equipaje**	*fahk-too-rahr ail ai-kee-pah-Gai*
to send in advance	**enviar delante**	*ain-vee-ahr dai-lahn-tai*
luggage ticket	**talón de equipaje**	*tah-lohn dai ai-kee-pah-Gai*
porter	**mozo**	*moh-thoh*
take our luggage to the train/boat	**lleve el equipaje al tren/barco**	*Lai-vai ail ai-kee-pah-Gai ahl train/bahr-koh*
to weigh	**pesar**	*pai-sahr*
to leave in left luggage	**dejar en consigna**	*dai-Gahr ain kohn-seeg-nah*
CUSTOMS	**la aduana**	*lah ah-doo-ah-nah*
customs officer	**el aduanero**	*ah-doo-ah-nai-roh*
customs inspection	**el vista de aduana**	*ail vees-tah dai ah-doo-ah-nah*

duty free	**libre de impuestos**	*lee-brai dai eem-poo-ais-tohs*
liable to duty	**expuesto a derechos**	*aix-pwai-stoh ah dai-rai-tshohs*
have you anything to declare?	**¿tiene algo que declarar?**	*tee-ai-nai ahl-goh kai dai-klah-rahr*
I have nothing to declare	**no tengo nada que declarar**	*noh tain-goh nah-dah kai dai-klah-rahr*
personal belongings	**efectos personales**	*ai-faik-tohs pair-soh-nah-lais*
Is there any duty to pay?	**¿hay algo que paga derechos?**	*ahee ahl-goh kai pah-gah dai-rai-tshohs*
How much do I have to pay?	**¿cuánto tengo que pagar?**	*koo-ahn-toh tain-goh kai pah-gahr*
What is in there?	**¿qué hay dentro?**	*kai ahee dain-troh*
Only my toilet things	**solo mis artículos de tocador**	*soh-loh mees ahr-tee-koo-lohs dai toh-kah-dohr*
These clothes have already been worn	**estas ropas han sido usadas**	*ais-tahs roh-pahs ahn see-doh oo-sah-dahs*

Be careful, please, these are breakable things	**cuidado por favor, estos equipajes son frágiles**	*koo-ee-dah-doh pohr fah-vohr, ais-tohs ai-kee-pah-Gais sohn frah-Gee-lais*

RAILWAY	**ferrocarril**	*fai-rroh-kah-rreel*

(see also Travelling, Luggage, Customs, Journey)

by rail	**por tren**	*pohr train*
the train stops	**el tren para**	*ail train pah-rah*
arrives	**llega**	*ail train Lai-gah*
fast train	**rápido**	*rah-pee-doh*
express train	**expreso**	*aix-prai-soh*
through train	**directo**	*dee-raik-toh*
to catch (miss) a train	**coger (perder) un tren**	*koh-Gair (pair-dair) oon train*
no need to change trains	**no hay que cambiar de tren**	*noh ah-ee kai kahm-bee-ahr dai train*
to make a connection	**transbordar/cambiar de tren**	*trans-bohr-dahr kahm-bee-ahr dai train*
station	**estación**	*ais-tah-thee-ohn*
booking office	**la taquilla**	*tah-kee-Lah*

waiting room	**sala de espera**	*sah-lah dai ais-pai-rah*
refreshment room	**el bar**	*bahr*
departure platform	**andén de salida**	*ahn-dain dai sah-lee-dah*
platform	**el andén**	*ahn-dain*
sleeping car (six berths in a compartment)	**coche-literas**	*koh-tshai – lee-tai-rahs*
sleeping car (individual accommodation with berth and basin)	**coche-cama**	*koh-tshai-kah-mah*
engine	**la locomotora**	*loh-koh-moh-toh-rah*
dining car	**restaurante**	*rais-tah-oo-rahn-tai*
this way for trains to . . .	**dirección . . .**	*dee-raik-thee-ohn*
corridor	**corredor**	*koh-rrai-dohr*
station master	**jefe de estación**	*Gai-fai dai ais-tah-thee-ohn*
ticket inspector	**el revisor**	*rai-vee-sohr*
guard	**el empleado**	*aimp-lai-ah-doh*

Is this the train for . . ?	**¿es este el tren para . .?**	*ais ais-tai ail train pah-rah*
compartment	**departamento**	*dai-pahr-tah-main-toh*
to open the window	**bajar la ventana**	*bah-Gahr lah vain-tah-nah*
Is this seat taken?	**¿está ocupado este asiento?**	*ais-tah oh-koo-pah-doh ais-tai ah-see-ain-toh*
There is no more room/seats	**no hay sitio**	*noh ahee see-tee-oh*
To turn off the heating	**quitar la calefacción**	*kee-tahr lah kah-lai-fahk-thee-ohn*
Do you mind if I smoke (open the window, shut the door?)	**¿le molesta si fumo, (bajo la ventana, cierro la puerta)?**	*lai moh-lais-tah see foo-moh (bah-Goh lah vain-tah-nah, thee-ai-roh lah poo-air-tah)*
What time do we arrive?	**¿a qué hora llegamos?**	*ah kai oh-rah Lai-gah-mohs*

The train is 15 mins late	**el tren tiene un retraso de quince minutos**	*ail train tee-ai-nai oon rai-trah-soh dai keen-thai mee-noo-tohs*

SHIPS	**barcos**	*bahr-kohs*

(see also 'At the seaside' P 137)

liners	**transatlánticos**	*trahns-aht-lahn-tee-kohs*
cruiser	**cruceros**	*kroo-thai-rohs*
sailing boat	**velero**	*vai-lai-roh*
rowing boat	**bote de remos**	*boh-tai dai rai-mohs*
fishing boat	**barco pesquero**	*bahr-koh pais-kai-roh*
cargo boat	**barco de carga**	*bahr-koh dai kahr-gah*
motor boat	**motora**	*moh-toh-rah*
yacht	**yate**	*yah-tai*
lifeboat	**bote salvavidas**	*boh-tai sahl-vah-vee-dahs*
life jacket	**chaleco salvavidas**	*tshah-lai-koh sahl-vah-vee-dahs*
port	**puerto**	*poo-air-toh*

maritime station	**estación marítima**	*ais-tah-thee-ohn mah-ree-tee-mah*
lighthouse	**faro**	*fah-roh*
out at sea	**en el mar**	*ain ail mahr*
sea sickness	**mareo**	*mah-rai-oh*
to embark	**embarcarse**	*aim-bahr-kahr-sai*
to land	**desembarcar**	*dais-aim-bahr-kahr*
the crossing	**la travesía**	*trah-vai-see-ah*
calm sea	**el mar quieto**	*mahr kee-ai-toh*
choppy sea	**el mar picado**	*mahr pee-kah-doh*
high sea	**el mar grueso**	*mahr groo-ai-soh*
rough sea	**el mar agitado**	*mahr ah-Gee-tah-doh*
the deck	**la cubierta**	*koo-bee-air-tah*
below deck	**bajo cubierta**	*bah-Goh koo-bee-air-tah*
the stern	**la popa**	*poh-pah*
the bow	**la proa**	*proh-ah*
berth	**litera**	*lee-tai-rah*
deck chair	**silla de cubierta**	*see-Lah dai koo-bee-air-tah*
the captain	**el capitán**	*kah-pee-tahn*

purser	**comisario de a bordo**	*koh-mee-sah-ree-oh dai ah bahr-doh*
steward	**sobre cargo**	*sob-rai kar-goh*
stewardess	**camarera**	*kah-mah-rai-rah*
sailor	**el marinero**	*mah-ree-nai-roh*
FLYING	**aviacíon**	*ah-vee-ah-thee-ohn*
to fly	**volar**	*voh-lahr*
aeroplane	**avión**	*ah-vee-ohn*
airport	**aeropuerto**	*ah-ai-roh-poo-air-toh*
by air	**por avión**	*pohr ah-vee-ohn*
runway	**la pista**	*pees-tah*
departure lounge	**sala de espera**	*sah-lah dai ais-pai-rah*
to take off	**despegar**	*dais-pai-gahr*
to climb	**subir**	*soo-beer*
to fly over	**trasvolar**	*trahs-voh-lahr*
to land	**aterrizar**	*ah-tai-rree-thahr*
speed	**velocidad**	*vai-loh-thee-dahd*
height	**altura**	*ahl-too-rah*
air hostess	**azafata**	*ah-thah-fah-tah*
air sickness	**mareo en el avión**	*mah-rai-oh ain ail ah-vee-ohn*
cotton wool	**algodón**	*ahl-goh-dohn*

something to drink	**algo de beber**	*ahl-goh dai bai-bair*
jumbo jets	**el jumbo**	(*as in English*)
charter flights	**vuelos de 'charter'**	*voo-ai-lohs dai 'tshahr-tair'*
scheduled flights	**vuelo normal**	*voo-ai-loh nohr-mahl*
helicopter	**helicóptero**	*ai-lee-kohp-tai-roh*
hovercraft	**hovercraft**	(*as in English*)
hand luggage	**equipaje de mano**	*ai-kee-pah-Gai dai mah-noh*
can I buy duty-free goods?	**¿Puedo hacer compras sin impuestos?**	*poo-ai-doh ah-thair kohm-prahs seen eem-poo-ais-tohs*
a saloon car	**un coche turismo**	*koh-tshai too-rees-moh*
a racing car	**un coche de sport**	*koh-tshai dai sporht*
beach buggy	**un cochecillo de playa**	*koh-chai-thee-yoh dai plah-yah*
motor cycle	**una motocicleta**	*moh-toh-thee-kleta*
driving licence (international)	**permiso de conducir (internacional)**	*pair-mee-soh dai kohn-doo-theer (een-tair-nah-thee-oh nahl)*

to start up	**arrancar**	*ah-rrahn-kahr*
to put into gear	**poner en cambio**	*poh-nair ain kahm-bee-oh*
full throttle, flat out	**al máximo**	*ahl mah-xee-moh*
to reverse	**poner la marcha atrás**	*poh-nair lah mahr-tshah ah-trahs*
to hoot	**tocar la bocina**	*toh-kahr lah bo-thee-nah*
to overtake	**adelantar**	*ah-dai-lahn-tahr*
to brake	**frenar**	*frai-nahr*
to accelerate	**acelerar**	*ah-thai-lai-rahr*
to slow down	**ir más despacio**	*eer mahs dais-pah-thee-oh*
to park	**aparcar**	*ah-pahr-kahr*
PETROL STATION	**una estación de servicio**	*ais-tah-thee-ohn dai sair-vee-thee-oh*
to fill up with petrol	**llenar de gasolina**	*Lai-nahr dai gah-soh-lee-nah*
to fill with water	**llenar de agua**	*Lai-nahr dai ah-gwah*
to fill with oil	**llenar de aceite**	*Lai-nahr dai ah-thai-ee-tai*

to change the oil	**cambiar el aceite**	*kahm-bee-ahr ail ah-thai-ee-tai*
to grease the car	**engrasar**	*ain-grah-sahr*
to wash the car	**lavar**	*lah-vahr*
to inflate the tyres	**inflar los neumáticos**	*een-flahr lohs nai-oo-mah-tee-kohs*
a spare can	**una lata de repuesto**	*lah-tah dai rai-poo-ais-toh*
REPAIR SHOP	**mecánica**	*mai-kah-nee-kah*
a breakdown	**una avería**	*ah-vai-ree-ah*
out of order	**no funcióna**	*noh foon-thee-oh nah*
broken	**roto**	*roh-toh*
burnt	**quemado**	*kai-mah-doh*
the choke	**el estrangulador**	*ais-trahn-goo-lah-dohr*
overheated	**caliente**	*kah-lee-ain-tai*
worn out	**usado**	*oo-sah-doh*
bent	**torcido**	*tohr-thee-doh*
repair	**reparar**	*rai-pah-rahr*
makes a funny noise	**hace un ruido extraño**	*ah-thai oon roo-ee-doh ais-trah-Noh*
to clear (a pipe etc.)	**destupir**	*dais-too-peer*

to change	**cambiar**	*kahm-bee-ahr*
to charge	**cargar**	*kahr-gahr*
to adjust	**arreglar**	*ah-rrai-glahr*
to tow in	**remolcar**	*rai-mohl kahr*
BODYWORK	**carrocería**	*kah-rroh-thai-ree-ah*
bonnet	**el capó**	*kah-poh*
hood	**la capota**	*kah-poh-tah*
door	**la puerta**	*poo-air-tah*
seat	**el asiento**	*ah-see-ain-toh*
window	**la ventanilla**	*vain-tah-nee-Lah*
headlights	**los faros**	*fah-rohs*
gear lever	**palanca de cambio**	*pah-lahn-kah dai kahm-bee-oh*
starter	**el arranque**	*ah-rrahn-kai*
horn	**la bocina**	*boh-thee-nah*
fog lamp	**faro de niebla**	*fah-roh dai nee-ai-blah*
steering wheel	**el volante**	*voh-lahn-tai*
springs	**los resortes**	*rai-sohr-tais*
brakes	**los frenos**	*frai-nohs*

dash-board	**tablero de instrumentos**	*tah-blai-roh dai eens-troo-main-tohs*
petrol tank	**el tanque de gasolina**	*tahn-kai dai gah-soh-lee-nah*
wheel	**la rueda**	*roo-ai-dah*
spare wheel	**la rueda de recambio**	*roo-ai-dah dai rai-kahm-bee-oh*
tyre	**el neumático**	*nai-oo-mah-tee-koh*
carburettor	**el carburador**	*kahr-boo-rah-dohr*
clutch	**el embrague**	*aim-brah-gai*
crankshaft	**el cigüeñal**	*thee-gwai-Nahl*
ignition	**el encendido**	*ain-thain-dee-doh*
magneto	**el magneto**	*mahg-nai-toh*
battery	**la batería**	*bah-tai-ree-ah*
starter motor	**motor de arranque**	*mohtoh dai arr-an-kai*
starting handle	**la manivela de arranque**	*mah-nee-vai-lah dai arr-an-kai*
sparking plugs	**las bujías**	*boo-Gee-ahs*
valve	**la válvula**	*vahl-voo-lah*

king pin	**pivote de dirección**	*pee-voh-tai dai dee-raik-thee-ohn*
oil pump	**bomba de aceite**	*bohm-bah dai ah-thai-eetai*

HOTELS

AT THE HOTEL	**en le hotel**	*ain ail oh-tail*
Which hotel would you recommend?	**¿Qué hotel podría usted recomendarme?**	*kai oh-tail poh-dree-ah oos-taid rai-koh-main-dahr-mai*
How much does full board per day cost?	**¿cuánto cuesta la pensión completa diaria?**	*koo-ahn-toh koo-ais-tah lah pain-see-ohn kohm-plai-tah dee-ah-ree-ah*
weekly (monthly)?	**¿semanal, (mensual)?**	*sai-mah-nal, (main-soo-ahl)*
a single room	**una habitación individual**	*ah-bee-tah-thee-ohn een dee-vee-doo-ahl*
a double room	**una habitación doble**	*ah-bee-tah-thee-ohn een dee-vee-doh-blai*
with private bath	**con baño**	*kohn bah-Noh*
with a basin only	**con lavabo solamente**	*kohn lah-vah-boh soh-lah-main-tai*

have my luggage sent up please	**haga subir mis maletas por favor**	*ah-gah soo-beer mees mah-lai-tahs pohr fah-vohr*
I will have this room	**me quedo con esta habitación**	*mai kai-doh kohn ais-tah ah-bee-tah-thee-ohn*
I would like to have a bath	**deseo tomar un baño**	*dai-sai-oh toh-mahr oon bah-Noh*
hall	**el recibidor**	*rai-thee-bee-dohr*
dining room	**el comedor**	*koh-mai-dohr*
bathroom	**el baño**	*bah-Noh*
lavatory	**el retrete**	*rai-trai-tai*
lift	**el ascensor**	*ahs-thain-sohr*
bell	**el timbre**	*teem-brai*
key	**la llave**	*Lah-vai*
manager	**el director**	*dee-raik-tohr*
porter, caretaker	**el portero**	*pohr-tai-roh*
receptionist	**el/la recepcionista**	*rai-thaip-thee-oh-nees-tah*
bill	**la cuenta**	*koo-ain-tah*
tip	**la propina**	*proh-pee-nah*

How much do I owe you?	**¿cuánto le debo?**	*koo-ahn-toh lai dai-boh*
Service included	**servicio incluido**	*sair-vee-thee-oh een-kloo-ee-doh*

ELECTRICITY

ELECTRICITY	**electricidad**	*ai-laik-tree-thee-dahd*
What is the voltage here?	**¿cuál es el voltaje aquí?**	*koo-ahl ais ail vohl-tah-Gai ah-kee*
the maximum is 220	**el máximo es doscientos veinte**	*ail mah-xee-moh ais dohs thee-ain-tohs vai-een-tai*
Do you have A.C. or D.C.?	**¿Tienen aquí corriente alterna o corriente continua?**	*tee-ai-nain ah-kee koh-rree-ain-tai ahl-tair-nah oh koh-rree-ain-tai kohn-tee-noo-ah*
plug	**el enchufe**	*aintshoo-fai*
do you have a fitting for my shaver (hair dryer, electric rollers)?	**Tiene un enchufe para mi máquina de afeitar (secador, rulos eléctricos)**	*tee-ain-ai oon ain-tshoo-fai pah-rah mee mah-kee-nah dai ah-fai-ee-tahr (sai-kah-dohr, roo-lohs ai-laik-tree-kohs)*

TOWN AND COUNTRY

IN THE TOWN	**En la ciudad**	*ain lah thee-oo-dahd*
an industrial town	**una ciudad industrial**	*oonah thee-oo-dahd een-doos-tree-ahl*
a commercial town	**comercial**	*oonah thee-oo-dahd koh-mair-thee-ahl*
a provincial town	**provincial**	*oonah thee-oo-dahd proh-veen-thee-ahl*
capital	**la capital**	*kah-pee-tahl*
inhabitants	**los habitantes**	*ah-bee-tahn-tais*
the centre of the town	**el centro de la ciudad**	*ail thain-troh dai lah thee-oo-dahd*
quarter; part of the town	**el barrio**	*bah-rree-oh*
the suburbs	**las afueras**	*ah-foo-ai-rahs*
main street	**calle principal**	*kah-Lai preen-thee-pahl*
side street	**calle lateral**	*kah-Lai lah-tai-rahl*

pavement	la acera	*ah-thai-rah*
roadway	la calzada	*kahl-thah-dah*
to cross the street	cruzar la calle	*kroo-thahr lah kah-Lai*
cross-roads	cruces	*kroo-thais*
at the corner	en la esquina	*ain lah ais-kee-nah*
square	la plaza	*plah-thah*
market (indoor)	el mercado (cubierto)	*mair-kah-doh (koo-bee-air-toh)*
bridge	el puente	*poo-ain-tai*
river	el río	*ree-oh*
church	la iglesia	*ee-glai-see-ah*
cathedral	la catedral	*kah-tai-drahl*
factory	la fábrica	*fah-bree-kah*
school	colegio OR escuela	*koh-lai-Gee-oh, ais-koo-ai-lah*
library	la biblioteca	*bee-blee-oh-tai-kah*
policeman	un guardia	*goo-ahr-dee-ah*
police-station	la comisaría de policía	*coh-mee-sah-ree-ah dai poh-lee-thee-ah*
fire-brigade	los bomberos	*bohm-bai-rohs*

bank	**el banco**	*bahn-koh*
hotel	**el hotel**	*oh-tail*
cinema	**el cine**	*thee-nai*
theatre	**el teatro**	*tai-ah-troh*
embassy	**la embajada**	*aim-bah-Gah-dah*
to go sight-seeing	**ir a ver los puntos de interés**	*eer ah vair lohs poon-tohs dai een-tai-rais*

El Sereno ail sai-rai-noh

If in Barcelona, Bilbao, Madrid, or any of the other main Spanish cities, and out later than 10.30 p.m. at night, you will almost certainly meet **el 'sereno'**. Every street has one, and this nightly worker, jangles from house to house with his chain of master keys locking up every front door. At about 6.30 a.m, he opens them all up, and clocks off for a day's rest. Should you find yourself with no outside door key, a slow hand clap will bring the **'sereno'** to your side to let you in – for a tip of about 5 pesetas. Hotels and Pensions usually have their own porter permanently at the door with a key in hand!

IN THE COUNTRY	**en el campo**	*ain ail kahm-poh*
small town	**un pueblo**	*poo-aibloh*
village	**una aldea**	*ahl-dai-ah*
farm	**una finca**	*feen-kah*
forest/wood	**un bosque**	*bohs-kai*
field	**un campo**	*kahm-poh*
meadow	**un prado**	*prah-doh*
stream	**un chorro**	*tshoh-rroh*
tree	**un árbol**	*ahr-bohl*
branch	**una rama**	*rah-mah*
flower	**una flor**	*flohr*
hill	**una colina**	*koh-lee-nah*
valley	**un valle**	*vah-Lai*
mountain	**una montaña**	*mohn-tah-Nah*
cottage	**una casita de campo**	*kah-see-tah dai kahm-poh*
barn	**un granero**	*grah-nai-roh*
orchard	**huerto**	*oo-air-toh*
kitchen garden	**huerta**	*oo-air-tah*
flower garden	**un jardín**	*Gahr-deen*
well	**un pozo**	*poh-thoh*

fountain	**una fuente**	*foo-ain-tai*
highway	**una carretera**	*kah-rai-tai-rah*
footpath	**senda para peatones**	*sain-dah pah-rah pai-ah-toh-nais*
pond	**un estanque**	*ais-tahn-kai*
lake	**un lago**	*lah-goh*
bird	**un pájaro**	*pah-Gah-roh*
wasp	**una avispa**	*ah-vees-pah*
bee	**una abeja**	*ah-bai-Gah*
mosquito	**un mosquito**	*mohs-kee-toh*

SEASIDE

AT THE SEASIDE	**al lado del mar**	*ahl lah-doh dail mahr*
(see also Ships P 119)		
beach	**la playa**	*plah-yah*
coast	**la costa**	*kohs-tah*
to swim	**nadar**	*nah-dahr*
bathing costume	**traje de baño**	*trah-Gai dai bah-Noh*
beach	**playa de baños**	*plah-yah dai bah-Nohs*
cap	**gorro de baño**	*goh-rroh dai bah-Noh*
trunks	**bañador**	*bah-Nah-dohr*
pier	**un muelle**	*moo-ai-Lai*
sand	**la arena**	*ah-rai-nah*
breakwater	**los rompeolas**	*rohm-pai-oh-lahs*
swimming	**natación**	*nah-tah-thee-ohn*
to swim across	**atravesar a nado**	*ah-trah-vai-sahr ah nah-doh*
high tide	**la marea alta**	*mah-rai-ah ahl-tah*
low tide	**baja**	*mah-rai-ah bah-Gah*

rocks	**las rocas**	*roh-kahs*
to fish	**pescar**	*pais-kahr*
waves	**las olas**	*oh-lahs*
swimming forbidden	**prohibido bañarse**	*proh-ee-bee-doh bah-Nahr-sai*

THE POST OFFICE

THE POST OFFICE	**oficina de correos**	*oh-fee-thee-nah dai koh-rrai-ohs*
Where is the nearest Post Office?	**¿Dónde está el correo, más cerca?**	*dohn-dai ais-tah ail koh-rrai-oh mahs thair-kah*
I want some stamps	**deseo unos sellos**	*dai-sai-oh oon-ohs sai-Lohs*
What is the postage to...?	**¿Cuánto es el franqueo para...?**	*koo-ahn-toh ais ail frahn-kai-oh pah-rah*
Three stamps	**tres sellos**	*trais sai-Lohs*
Five postcards, please	**cinco postales por favor**	*theen-koh pohs-tah-lais pohr fah-vohr*
To send a telegram	**mandar un telegrama**	*mahn-dahr oon tai-lai-grah-mah*
What is the charge per word?	**¿Cuánto vale por palabra?**	*koo-ahn-toh vah-lai pohr pah-lah-brah*

Reply prepaid	**con contestación pagado**	*kohn Kon-test-ah-thee-on pah-gah-doh*
I want to register this letter	**Quiero certificar esta carta**	*kee-ai-roh thair-tee-fee-kahr ais-tah kahr-tah*
Are there any letters for me?	**¿hay cartas para mí?**	*ah-ee kahr-tahs pah-rah mee*
Please forward my letters to this address	**Por favor mande mis cartas a esta dirección**	*pohr fah-vohr mahn-dai mees kahr-tahs ah ais-tah dee-raik-thee-ohn*
Air mail	**por avión**	*pohr ah-vee-ohn*
letter box	**un buzón**	*boo-thohn*
a money order	**un giro**	*Gee-roh*
parcel	**un paquete**	*pah-kai-tai*
registered letter	**una carta certificada**	*kah-tah thair-tee-fee-kah-dah*
envelope	**un sobre**	*soh-brai*
printed matter	**impresos**	*eem-prai-sohs*

THE TELEPHONE

TELEPHONE	**teléfono**	*tai-lai-foh-noh*
to telephone	**llamar por teléfono**	*Lah-mahr pohr tai lai-foh-noh*
telephone number	**número de teléfono**	*noo-mai-roh dai-lai-foh-noh*
telephone directory	**guía telefónica**	*gee-ah tai-lai-foh-nee-kah*
I wish to telephone to London	**deseo una conferencia con Londrés**	*dai-sai-oh oonah kohn-fai-rain-thee-ah kohn lohn-drais*
to hang up the receiver	**colgar el aparato**	*kohl-gahr ail ah-pah-rah-toh*
to pick up the receiver	**descolgar el aparato**	*dais-kohl-gahr ail ah-pah-rah-toh*

Connect me with Madrid 276-15-73	póngame una conferencia con Madrid dos siete seis, uno cinco, siete tres	*pohn-gah-mai oonah kohn-fai-rain-thee-ah kohn Mah-dreed dohs see-ai-tai sai-ees, oonoh theen-koh, see-ai-tai tra is*
the line is engaged	la línea está ocupada	*lah lee-nai-ah ais-tah oh-koo-pah-dah*
the line is now free	ya está la línea desocupada	*yah ais-tah lah lee-nai-ah dai-soh-koo-pah-dah*
Are you there Mr. B...?	¿oiga está el señor B...?	*oh-ee-gah, ais-tah ail sai-Nohr*
He's not here; this is ... speaking	no está, soy ...	*noh aistah; soh-ee*
I would like to speak to ...	quiero hablar con	*kee-ai-roh ah-blahr kohn*
There is a waiting time of an hour	hay una demora de una hora	*ah-ee oonah dai-moh-rah dai oonah oh-rah*

a person to person call	**una conferencia de persona a persona**	*oo-nah kohn-fai-rain thee-ah dai pair-soh-nah ah pair-soh-nah*

1. Public telephone boxes (**cabina de teléfono** – *kah-bee-nah dai tai-lai-foh-noh*), are usually grey, and can only be used for local calls, using one peseta coins. Lift the receiver, and wait for a continuous tone. Insert three pesetas (3 mins.) and dial the number. The money automatically registers when the call is answered. The engaged signal is similar to England (short intermittent pips) – not to be confused with the 'ringing' sound, which is a series of LONG intermittent tones. Most bars and restaurants also have public telephones that generally function with a special disc – **'una ficha'** – *fee-tshah* – Worth three pesetas, it is usually obtainable from the waiters or cloakroom assistant.

2. For long distant calls – either in Spain or abroad, every town has a **'Central de teléfonos'** – *thain-trahl dai tai-lai-foh-nohs* – The operator at the desk will connect you, the cost of the call is immediately registered, and you pay on the way out.

THE RESTAURANT

THE RESTAURANT	**el restaurante**	*rais-tah-oo-rahn-tai*
grill room	**la parrilla**	*pah-rreeLah*
waiter/waitress	**camarero/a**	*kah-mah-rai-roh/ah*
table for two	**una mesa para dos**	*mai-sah pah-rah dohs*
to reserve a table	**reservar una mesa**	*rai-sair-vahr oonah mai-sah*
the menu	**la carta, el menú**	*kahr-tah; mai-noo*
wine list	**lista de vinos**	*lees-tah dai vee-nohs*
table d'hôte	**menú del día**	*mai-noo dail dee-ah*
special dishes	**platos especiales**	*plah-tohs esp-eth-ee-ah-lais*
Can you recommend this?	**¿puede recomendarme esto?**	*poo-ai-dai rai-koh-main-dahr-mai ais-toh*
Anything more for you?	**¿algo más, señores?**	*ahl-goh mahs sai-Noh-rais*

a knife (fork, spoon) is missing	me hace falta un cuchillo (tenedor, cuchara)	*mai ah-thai fahl-tah oon koo-tshee-Loh (tai-nai-dohr, koo-tshah-rah)*
take this away please	llévese esto por favor	*Lai-vai-sai ais-toh pohr fah-vohr*
It is not fresh (clean)	no es fresco (limpio)	*noh ais frais-koh (leem-pee-oh)*
Waiter, the bill please	oiga, la cuenta por favor	*oh-ee-gah, lah koo-ain-tah pohr fah-vohr*
Keep the change	guarde el cambio	*goo-ahr-dai ail kahm-bee-oh*
fork	tenedor	*tai-nai-dohr*
knife	cuchillo	*koo-tshee-Loh*
spoon	cuchara	*koo-tsha-rah*
plate	un plato	*plah-toh*
napkin	una servilleta	*sair-vee-Lai-tah*
salt	sal	*sahl*
pepper	pimienta	*pee-mee-ain-tah*
oil	aceite	*ah-thai-ee-tai*

vinegar	**vinagre**	*vee-nah-grai*
a portion	**una porción**	*pohr-thee-ohn*
a meal	**una comida**	*koh-mee-dah*
to have breakfast/ lunch/tea/dinner	**desayunar/comer/ merendar/cenar**	*dai-sah-yoo-nahr/ koh-mair/mai-rain-dahr/thai-nahr*
breakfast	**el desayuno**	*dai-sah-yoo-noh*
lunch	**la comida, el almuerzo**	*koh-mee-dah, ahl-moo-air-thoh*
tea	**la merienda**	*mai-ree-ain-dah*
dinner	**la cena**	*thai-nah*

Note: The different foods are given below so that you can ask for what you want, whether at a restaurant or at a shop. If you are confronted with a Spanish menu, consult the alphabetical menu translator which begins on page 95.

DESAYUNO breakfast

milky coffee	**café con leche**	*kah-fai kohn lai-tshai*
black coffee	**café solo**	*kah-fai soh-loh*
black with a dash	**un cortado**	*kohr-tah-doh*
iced coffee	**café con hielo**	*kah-fai kohn ee-ai-loh*

Note: Coffee in Spain is drunk very strong, frequently and in small amounts – if you're used to a large cup of coffee, ask for a double – **un doble** – *doh-blai*

toast	**pan tostado**	*pahn tohs-tah-doh*
rusks	**bizcochos**	*beeth-koh-tshohs*
sweet breakfast bun	**una magdalena**	*mahg-dah-lai-nah*
hot chocolate	**un chocolate a la francesa**	*tshoh-koh-lah-tai ah lah frahn-thai-sah*
hot/cold milk	**leche caliente/fría**	*lai-tshai kah-lee-ain-tai/free-ah*
tea	**un té**	*tai*
finger sized strips of puffed fried pancake batter	**churros**	*tshoo-rrohs*
cheese/ham roll	**un bocadillo de queso/jamón**	*boh-kah-dee-Loh dai kai-soh/Gah-mohn*
omelette	**una tortilla**	*tohr-tee-Lah*
fried eggs	**huevos fritos**	*oo-ai-vohs free-tohs*
butter	**mantequilla**	*mahn-tai-kee-Lah*
jam	**mermelada**	*mair-mai-lah-dah*
marmalade	**mermelada de naranja**	*mair-mai-lah-dah dai nah-rahn-Gah*

sugar	**azucar**	*ah-thoo-kahr*
LUNCH/DINNER	**la comida/la cena**	*koh-mee-dah/thai-nah*
apple	**manzana**	*mahn-thah-nah*
apricot	**albaricoque**	*ahl-bah-ree-koh-kai*
artichoke	**alcachofa**	*ahl-kah-tshoh-fah*
asparagus	**espárrago**	*ais-pah-rrah-goh*
banana	**plátano**	*plah-tah-noh*
bacon	**tocino**	*toh-thee-noh*
beans, green	**judías verdes**	*Goo-dee-ahs vair-dais*
broad	**habas**	*ah-bahs*
butter	**judías blancas**	*Goo-dee-ahs blahn-kahs*
beef	**vaca**	*vah-kah*
bread	**pan**	*pahn*
breast (of fowl)	**la pechuga**	*pai-tshoo-gah*
broth (thin soup)	**caldo**	*kahl-doh*
brains	**sesos**	*sai-sohs*
brussel sprouts	**col de Bruselas**	*kohl dai broo-sai-lahs*
biscuits	**bizcochos**	*beeth-koh-tshohs*
cabbage	**col**	*kohl*

cake	un dulce	*dool-thai*
carrot	zanahoria	*thah-nah-oh-ree-ah*
cauliflower	coliflor	*koh-lee-flohr*
celery	ápio	*ah-pee-oh*
caramel custard	flan	*flahn*
cheese	queso	*kai-soh*
chop	una chuleta	*tshoo-lai-tah*
clams	almejas	*ahl-mai-Gahs*
cold meats	fiambres	*fee-ahm-brais*
crab	cangrejo	*kahn-grai-Goh*
cucumber	pepino	*pai-pee-noh*
duck	pato	*pah-toh*
eel	anguila	*ahn-gee-lah*
egg, fried	huevo, frito	*oo-ai-voh, free-toh*
hard	duro	*oo-ai-voh, doo-roh*
boiled	pasado por agua	*pah-sah-doh pohr ah-goo-ah*
scrambled	revueltos	*rai-voo-ail-tohs*
poached	escalfado	*ais-kahl-fah-doh*
fish	pescado	*pais-kah-doh*
fillet of	filete de	*fee-lai-tai dai*

game	**caza**	*kah-thah*
garlic	**ajo**	*ah-Goh*
grapes	**uvas**	*oo-vahs*
ham	**jamón**	*Gah-mohn*
herrings	**arenques**	*ah-rain-kais*
honey	**miel**	*mee-ail*
hake	**merluza**	*mair-loo-thah*
jam	**mermelada**	*mair-mai-lah-dah*
ice cream	**helado**	*ai-lah-doh*
kidneys	**riñones**	*ree-Noh-nais*
lamb	**cordero**	*kohr-dai-roh*
lemon	**limón**	*lee-mohn*
lettuce	**lechuga**	*lai-tshoo-gah*
liver	**hígado**	*ee-gah-doh*
lobster	**langosta**	*lahn-gohs-tah*
loin of	**lomo de**	*loh-moh dai*
mackerel	**caballa**	*kah-bah-Lah*
meat	**carne**	*kahr-nai*
melon	**melón**	*mai-lohn*
minced meat	**carne picada**	*kahr-nai pee-kah-dah*
milk	**leche**	*lai-tshai*

mushrooms	setas	*sai-tahs*
mussels	mejillones	*mai-Gee-Loh-nais*
macaroni	macarrones	*mah-kah-rroh-nais*
mustard	mostaza	*mohs-tah-thah*
nuts	nueces	*noo-ai-thais*
walnut	nuez de nogal	*noo-aith dai noh-gahl*
onion	cebolla	*thai-boh-Lah*
orange	naranja	*nah-rahn-Gah*
oyster	ostras	*ohs-trahs*
octopus	pulpo	*pool-poh*
parsley	perejil	*pai-rai-Geel*
paté	paté	*pah-tai*
peach	melocotón	*mai-loh-koh-tohn*
pear	pera	*pai-rah*
peas	guisantes	*gee-sahn-tais*
pheasant	faisán	*fah-ee-sahn*
prawns	langostinos	*lahn-gohs-tee-nohs*
pork	cerdo	*thair-doh*
pigeon	paloma	*pah-loh-mah*
young pigeon	pichón	*pee-tshohn*
potatoes, fried	patatas fritas	*pah-tah-tahs free-tahs*

mashed	**puré de patatas**	*poo-rai dai pah-tah-tahs*
boiled	**patatas cocidas**	*koh-thee-dahs*
pineapple	**piña**	*pee-Nah*
poultry	**aves**	*ah-vais*
quail	**codorniz**	*koh-dohr-neeth*
radish	**rábano**	*rah-bah-noh*
rice	**arroz**	*ah-rrohth*
raspberry	**frambuesa**	*frahm-boo-ai-sah*
ravioli	**ravioli**	*rah-vee-oh-lee*
rabbit	**conejo**	*koh-nai-Goh*
roast . . .	**asado**	*ah-sah-doh*
salad	**ensalada**	*ain-sah-lah-dah*
salmon	**salmón**	*sahl-mohn*
sausage	**salchicha**	*sahl-tshee-tshah*
shrimps	**gambas**	*gahm-bahs*
squid	**calamares**	*kah-lah-mah-rais*
soup	**sopa**	*soh-pah*
spinach	**espinacas**	*ais-pee-nah-kahs*
stew (pork and butter beans)	**fabada**	*fah-bah-dah*

sweet (pudding)	el postre	*pohs-trai*
strawberry	fresa	*frai-sah*
sweetbreads	mollejas	*moh-Lai-Gahs*
split peas	lentejas	*lain-tai-Gahs*
sardines	sardinas	*sahr-dee-nahs*
tomato	tomate	*toh-mah-tai*
tongue	lengua	*lain-gwah*
trout	trucha	*troo-tshah*
turkey	pavo	*pah-voh*
tripe	callos	*kah-Lohs*
tunny fish	atún	*ah-toon*
veal	ternera	*tair-nai-rah*
vegetables	verduras	*vair-doo-rahs*

DRINKS

The cheapest drink of course is wine. It is sometimes pretty rough and frequently drunk with clear fizzy water (**gaseosa**), particularly at lunchtime when there's work to be done in the afternoon!

'**Sangría**' is the famous wine cup. Well worth trying, and consists mainly of red wine, clear fizzy lemon, sliced fruits and gin, with brandy or rum to give it a kick. No two Spaniards make it alike, so try it in different places, though check the price before ordering – considering how cheap wine and brandy are in Spain, prices for '**Sangría**' are often out of all proportion to reality!

Bottled water is more expensive than wine, and unless you're in a particularly suspect looking restaurant, out of the main tourist spots, the tap water won't harm you. Lastly, if you are unfortunate enough to have an upset tum – through drink or food – the Spanish cure is a day in bed with a litre bottle of fizzy water (**agua con gas**) to drink!

DRINKS	**bebidas**	*bai-bee-dahs*
(for coffee, milk, tea see p. 146–147)		
a glass of . . .	**un vaso de . . .**	*oon vah-soh dai*
a cup of . . .	**una taza de . . .**	*oo-nah tah-thah dai*
let's go and have a drink	**vamos a tomar una copa**	*vah-mohs ah toh-mahr oo-nah koh-pah*
coffee	**café**	*kah-fai*
water (mineral)	**agua mineral**	*ah-gwah mee-nairahl*
fizzy or still	**con gas o sin gas**	*kohn gahs oh seen gahs*
clear fizzy lemonade	**gaseosa de limon**	*gah-sai-oh-sah dai lee-mohn*
lemon squash	**limonada**	*lee-moh-nah-dah*
orange squash	**naranjada**	*nah-rahn-Gah-dah*
fresh lemon (orange)	**limón (naranja) natural**	*lee-mohn (nah-rahn-Gah) nah-too-rahl*
orange (pineapple) juice	**zumo de naranja (piña)**	*thoo-moh dai nah-rahn-Gah (pee-Nah)*
beer	**cerveza**	*thair-vai-thah*
½ pint (approx)	**una caña**	*kah-Nah*
1 pint (approx)	**una caña doble**	*kah-Nah doh-blai*
shandy	**una caña clara**	*kah-Nah clah-rah*

cider	**sidra**	*see-drah*
ice	**hielo**	*ee-ai-loh*
wine (red, rose, white)	**vino (tinto, rosado, blanco)**	*vee-noh (teen-toh roh-sah-doh, blahn-koh)*
rum	**ron**	*rohn*
rum and coke	**un cubalibre**	*koo-bah-lee-brai*
coca cola	**una coca-cola**	*koh-kah-koh-lah*
gin and tonic	**una ginebra con tónica**	*Gee-nai-brah kohn toh-nee-kah*
gin and coke	**un cubalibre de ginebra**	*koo-bah-lee-brai dai Gee-nai-brah*
vermouth and soda	**un vermut con soda**	*vair-moot kohn soh-dah*
whisky and soda	**whisky and soda**	*whisky con soda*
sangria	**sangría**	*sahn-gree-ah* (*see p* 154)

SHOPS

SHOPS AND SHOPPING	**tiendas y compras**	*tee-ain-dahs ee kohm-prahs*
shop	**la tienda**	*tee-ain-dah*
department store	**grandes almacenes**	*grahn-dais ahl-mah-thai-nais*
supermarket	**supermercado**	*soo-pair-mair-kah-doh*
to buy	**comprar**	*kohm-prahr*
to sell	**vender**	*vain-dair*
shoe department	**zapatería**	*thah-pah-tai-ree-ah*
shop assistant	**el dependiente**	*dai-pain-dee-ain-tai*
shop keeper	**el tendero**	*tain-dai-roh*
the 'sales'	**las rebajas**	*rai-bah-Gahs*
price	**precio**	*prai-thee-oh*
manager	**el jefe**	*Gai-fai*
what can I do for you? what would you like?	**¿qué quiere usted?**	*kai kee-ai-rai oos-taid*
anything else?	**¿algo más?**	*ahl-goh mahs*

I want to buy some soap	**quiero comprar jabón**	*kee-ai-roh kohm-prahr Ga-bohn*
do you have any razor blades?	**¿tiene hojitas de afeitar?**	*tee-ai-nai oh-Gee-tahs dai ah-fai-ee-tahr*
how many do you want?	**¿cuántos quiere usted?**	*koo-ahn-tohs kee-ai-rai oos-taid*
half a dozen please	**media docena por favor**	*mai-dee-ah doh-thai-nah pohr fah-vohr*
how much does it cost?	**¿cuánto vale OR cuánto cuesta?**	*koo-ahn-to vah-lai koo-ais-tah*
it is too big	**es demasiado grande**	*ais dai-mah-see-ah-doh grahn-dai*
small	**pequeño**	*ais dai-mah-see-ah-doh pai-kai-No*
wide	**ancho**	*ais dai-mah-see-ah-doh ahn-tshoh*
narrow	**estrecho**	*ais dai-mah-see-ah-doh ais-trai-tshoh*
thin, fine	**fino**	*ais dai-mah-see-ah-doh fee-noh*

it is too expensive	**es demasiado caro**	*ais dai-mah-see-ah-doh kah-roh*
it is too cheap	**es demasiado barato**	*ais dai-mah-see-ah-doh bah-rah-toh*
it is too long	**es demasiado largo**	*ais dai-mah-see-ah-doh lahr-goh*
it is too short	**es demasiado corto**	*ais dai-mah-see-ah-doh kohr-toh*
do you have anything bigger?	**¿tiene algo más grande?**	*tee-ai-nai ahl-goh mahs grahn-dai*
do you have anything cheaper?	**¿tiene algo más barato?**	*tee-ai-nai ahl-goh mahs bah-rah-toh*
can you change this note for me?	**¿puede cambiarme este billete?**	*poo-ai-dai kahm-bee-ahr-mai ais-tai bee-Lai-tai*
do you accept credit cards?	**¿aceptan ustedes tarjetas de crédito?**	*ah-thaip-tahn oos-tai-dais tahr-Gai-tahs dai crai-dee-toh*
do you have any identification?	**¿tiene usted documento de identidad?**	*tee-ai-nai oos-taid doh-koo-main-toh dai ee-dain-tee-dahd*

COLOURS	colores	*koh-loh-rais*
black	negro/a	*nai-groh/ah*
blue (navy, sky)	azul (marino, celeste)	*ah-thool (mah-ree-noh, thai-lais-tai)*
brown	marrón	*mah-rrohn*
green	verde	*vair-dai*
yellow	amarillo/a	*ah-mah-ree-Loh/ah*
red	rojo/a	*roh-Goh/ah*
pink	rosa	*roh-sah*
orange	naranja	*nah-rahn-Gah*
grey	gris	*grees*
white	blanco/a	*blahn-koh/ah*
mauve	violeta	*vee-oh-lai-tah*
cream	crema	*crai-mah*
clear	claro/a	*clah-roh/ah*
dark	oscuro/a	*ohs-koo-roh/ah*
Baker	panadería	*pahn-ah-dai-ree-ah*
bread	pan	*pahn*
roll	panecillo	*pahn-ai-thee-Loh*
tin loaf	pan de molde	*pahn dai mohl-dai*

sweet dry bun	**magdelena**	*mahg-dai-lai-nah*
cresent shaped roll	**croisant**	*kroh-ee-sahnt*
dry toast	**bizcocho**	*beeth-koh-tshoh*
Bank	**el banco**	*bahn-koh*
foreign exchange office	**cambio de dinero**	*kahm-bee-oh dai dee-nai-roh*
money	**dinero**	*dee-nai-roh*
to change	**cambiar**	*kahm-bee-ahr*
bank note (of 1,000 pesetas)	**un billete (de mil pesetas)**	*bee-Lai-tai (dai meel pai-sai-tahs)*
small change	**moneda**	*moh-nai-dah*
rate of exchange	**tipo de cambio**	*tee-poh dai kahm-bee-oh*
American dollars	**dólares americanos**	*doh-lah-rais, ah-mai-ree-kah-nohs*
a pound	**una libra**	*lee-brah*
traveller's cheque	**cheque de viaje**	*tshai-kai dai vee-ah-Gai*
receipt	**un recibo**	*rai-thee-boh*

to pay cash	**pagar al contado**	*pah-gahr ahl kohn-tah-doh*
to cash a cheque	**cobrar un cheque**	*koh-brahr oon tshai-kai*

Note: Spanish money is divided in the following way:

Notes	Change
1,000 pesetas	100 peseta piece
500 pesetas	50 peseta piece
100 pesetas	25 peseta piece
	5 peseta piece
	1 peseta piece
	50 centimes
	(100 centimes = 1 peseta)
	10 centimes

Bookshop	**librería**	*lee-brai-ree-ah*
book	**libro**	*lee-broh*
dictionary	**diccionario**	*deek-thee-oh-nah-ree-oh*
a guide book of . . .	**una guía sobre . . .**	*gee-ah soh-brai*

a map	un mapa	*mah-pah*
Bootmaker	zapatería	*thah-pah-tai-ree-ah*
boots	botas	*boh-tahs*
shoes	zapatos	*thah-pah-tohs*
sandals	sandalias	*sahn-dah-lee-ahs*
to mend	reparar	*rai-pah-rahr*
to sole	poner una suela	*poh-nair oo-nah soo-ai-lah*
to heel	poner un tacón	*poh-nair oon tah-kohn*
high heel shoe	zapato de tacón alto	*thah-pah-toh dai tah-kohn ahl-toh*
low heel shoe	bajo	*thah-pah-toh dai tah-kohn bah-Goh*
shoe polish	betún	*bai-toon*
street shoe cleaner	limpiabotas	*leem-pee-ah-boh-tahs*
laces	cordones	*kohr-doh-nais*
Butcher	carnicería	*kahr-nee-thai-ree-ah*
meat	carne	*kahr-nai*
fillets	filetes	*fee-lai-tais*
minced	picado	*pee-kah-doh*
in chunks	en trozitos	*ain troh-thee-tohs*

Chemist	**droguería**	*droh-gai-ree-ah*
soap	**jabón**	*Gah-bohn*
razor	**navaja de afeitar**	*nah-vah-Gah dai ah-fai-ee-tahr*
razor blade	**hojita de afeitar**	*oh-Gee-tah dai ah-fai-ee-tahr*
hair lotion	**colonia para el pelo**	*koh-loh-nee-ah pah-rah ail pai-loh*
nail file	**una lima**	*lee-mah*
lipstick	**lápiz de labios**	*lah-peeth dai lah-bee-ohs*
face powder	**polvos**	*pohl-vohs*
deodorant	**desodorante**	*dai-soh-doh-rahn-tai*
talcum powder	**polvo de talco**	*pohl-voh dai tahl-koh*
face cream	**crema para la cara**	*crai-mah pah-rah lah kah-rah*
toothbrush	**cepillo de dientes**	*thai-pee-Loh dai dee-ain-tais*
toothpaste	**pasta de dientes**	*pahs-tah dai dee-ain-tais*
clothes pegs	**pinzas**	*peen-thahs*

comb	**peine**	*pai-ee-nai*
brush	**cepillo**	*thai-pee-Loh*
tanning lotion	**bronceador**	*brohn-thai-ah-dohr*
Dispensing chemist	**farmacia**	*fahr-mah-thee-ah*
aspirin	**aspirina**	*ahs-pee-ree-nah*
vaseline	**vaselina**	*vah-sai-lee-nah*
sedative/pain killer	**calmante**	*kahl-mahn-tai*
cotton wool	**algodón**	*ahl-goh-dohn*
bandage	**una venda**	*vain-dah*
iodine	**tinta de yodo**	*teen-tah dai yo-doh*
bicarbonate of soda	**bicarbonato**	*bee-kahr-boh-nah-toh*
laxative	**un laxante**	*lah-xahn-tai*
purgative	**un purgante**	*poor-gahn-tai*
sanitary towel	**paño higiénico**	*pah-Noh ee-Gee-ai-nee-koh*
castor oil	**aceite de ricino**	*ah-thai-ee-tai de ree-thee-noh*
Camera shop	**una tienda de cámaras**	*tee-ain-dah dai kah-mah-rahs*
camera	**máquina fotográfica**	*mah-kee-nah foh-toh grah-fee-kah*

film	**un rollo**	*roh-Loh*
colour or black and white?	**¿de color o negro y blanco?**	*dai koh-lohr oh nai-groh ee blahn-koh*
35 mm film	**rollo de trienta y cinco milímetros**	*roh-Loh dai trai-een-tah ee theen-koh mee-lee-mai-trohs*
flash bulb	**un flash**	flash (same as in English)
can you mend this camera?	**¿puede usted reparar esta máquina?**	*poo-ai-dai oos-taid rai-pah-rahr ais-tah mah-kee-nah*
can you enlarge this photo?	**¿puede usted ampliar esta foto?**	*poo-ai-dai oos-taid ahm-plee-ahr ais-tah foh-toh*
photocopy	**fotocopia**	*foh-toh-coh-pee-ah*
Confectioner's and cake shop	**bombonería y pastelería**	*bohm-bohn-ee-re-ah ee pahst-ai-lee-ree-ah*
chocolate	**chocolate**	*tshoh-koh-lah-tai*
sweets	**caramelos**	*kah-rah-mai-lohs*
toffees	**tofe**	*toh-fai*
chewing gum	**chicle**	*tshee-klai*

sugared almonds	**peladillas**	*pai-lah-dee-Lahs*
cream	**nata**	*nah-tah*
Dairy	**lechería**	*lai-tshai-ree-ah*
milk	**leche**	*lai-tshai*
yoghourt	**yoghourt**	(*same as English*)
butter	**mantequilla**	*mahn-tai-kee-Lah*
margarine	**margarina**	*mahr-gah-ree-nah*
Drapery	**mercería**	*mair-thai-ree-ah*
dress material	**tela**	*tai-lah*
scissors	**tijeras**	*tee-Gai-rahs*
cotton	**algodón**	*ahl-goh-dohn*
needle	**aguja**	*ah-goo-Gah*
pin	**alfiler**	*ahl-fee-lair*
thread	**hilo**	*ee-loh*
Dry cleaner's	**tintorería**	*teen-toh-rai-ree-ah*
to clean	**limpiar**	*leem-pee-ahr*
to dye	**teñir**	*tai-Neer*
to press	**planchar**	*plahn-tshahr*

Fishmonger's	**pescadería**	*pais-kah-dai-ree-ah*
fish	**pescado**	*pais-kah-doh*
Fruit and greengrocer's	**frutería**	*froo-tai-ree-ah*
fruit	**fruta**	*froo-tah*
vegetables	**verduras**	*vair-doo-rahs*
Grocer's	**tienda de ultramarinos**	*tee-ain-dah dai ool-trah-mah-ree-nohs*
Hairdresser's	**peluquería**	*pai-loo-kai-ree-ah*
a hair cut	**un corte de pelo**	*oon kohr-tai dai pai-loh*
not too short	**no demasiado corto**	*noh dai-mah-see-ah-doh kohr-toh*
fairly short	**bastante corto**	*bahs-tahn-tai kohr-toh*
longer at the back	**más largo por detrás**	*mahs lahr-goh pohr dai-trahs*
shorter here	**más corto por aquí**	*mahs kohr-toh pohr ah-kee*
a wash and set	**lavar y marcar**	*lah-vahr ee mahr-kahr*

hair setting lotion	**un fijador**	*oon fee-Gah-dohr*
conditioner	**acondicionador**	*ah-kohn-dee-thee-oh-nah-dohr*
brilliantine	**brillantina**	*bree-Lahn-tee-nah*
hair spray	**laca**	*lah-kah*
a manicure	**una manicura**	*mah-nee-koo-rah*
to remove hair on legs	**depilar las piernas**	*dai-pee-lahr lahs pee-air-nahs*
a wash and dry only	**lavar y secar solamente**	*lah-vahr ee sai-kahr soh-lah main-tai*
Jeweller's	**jollería**	*Goh-Lai-ree-ah*
natural stones	**piedras naturales**	*pee-ai-drahs nah-too-rah-lais*
semi-precious stones	**piedras semipreciosas**	*pee-ai-drahs sai-mee-prai thee-oh-sahs*
bracelet	**un brazalete**	*brah-thah-lai-tai*
brooch	**un broche**	*broh-tshai*
ear-ring	**un pendiente**	*pain-dee-ain-tai*
ring	**una sortija**	*sohr-tee-Gah*
tie pin	**un alfiler de corbata**	*ahl-fee-lair dai kohr-bah-tah*

cuff links	**gemelos**	*Gai-mai-lohs*
necklace	**un collar**	*koh-Lahr*
wedding ring	**anillo de boda**	*ah-nee-Loh dai boh-dah*
gold	**oro**	*oh-roh*
silver	**plata**	*plah-tah*
platinum	**platino**	*plah-tee-noh*
diamond	**diamante**	*dee-ah-mahn-tai*
emerald	**esmeralda**	*ais-mai-rahl-dah*
pearl	**perla**	*pair-lah*
ruby	**rubí**	*roo-bee*
Poultry and egg shop	**pollería y huevería**	*poh-Lai-ree-ah ee oo-ai-vai-ree-ah*
chicken	**pollo**	*poh-Loh*
a dozen eggs	**una docena de huevos**	*oo-nah doh-thai-nah dai oo-ai-vohs*
hen	**gallina**	*gah-Lee-nah*
cock	**gallo**	*gah-Loh*
Stationer's	**papelería**	*pah-pai-lai-ree-ah*
pencil	**un lápiz**	*lah-peeth*

fountain pen	**una pluma**	*ploo-mah*
pad of paper	**un bloc**	*blohk*
airmail paper	**papel de avión**	*pah-pail dai ah-vee-ohn*
envelopes	**sobres**	*soh-brais*
post card	**una postal**	*pohs-tahl*
biro	**un bolígrafo**	*boh-lee-grah-foh*
Tobacconist	**un estanco**	*ais-tahn-koh*
tobacco	**tabaco**	*tah-bah-koh*
cigarette	**cigarillos**	*thee-gah-reeLohs*
cigar	**un puro**	*poo-roh*
matches	**cerillas**	*thai-reeLahs*
pipe	**una pipa**	*pee-pah*
lighter	**un mechero**	*mai-tshai-roh*
flints	**piedra para el mechero**	*pee-ai-drah pah-rah ail mai-tshai-roh*
stamps	**sellos**	*sai-Lohs*

Note: In Spain the 'estancos' are government controlled and are easily distinguishable by their red and yellow striped frontage.

Watchmakers	**relojería**	*rai-loh-Gai-ree-ah*
watch	**reloj de pulsera**	*rai-lohG dai pool-sai-rah*
clock	**reloj**	*rai-lohG*
alarm clock	**despertador**	*dais-pair-tah-dohr*
automatic	**automático**	*ah-oo-toh-mah-tee-koh*
it is fast	**está adelantado**	*ais-tah ah-dai-lahn-tah-doh*
it is slow	**está atrasado**	*ais-tah ah-trah-sah-doh*
Ladies clothes	**ropa para señoras**	*roh-pah pah-rah sai-Noh-rahs*
bra	**sujetador**	*soo-Gai-tah-dohr*
briefs	**bragas**	*brah-gahs*
petticoat	**combinación**	*kohm-bee-nah-thee-ohn*
coat	**abrigo**	*ah-bree-goh*
cardigan	**rebeca**	*rai-bah-kah*
dress	**un vestido**	*vais-tee-doh*
blouse	**una blusa**	*bloo-sah*

shirt	**una camisa**	*kah-mee-sah*
jumper/jersey	**un jersey**	*Gair-sai-ee*
suit	**un traje**	*trah-Gai*
trousers	**pantalones**	*pahn-tah-loh-nais*
skirt	**una falda**	*fahl-dah*
nightdress	**un camisón**	*kah-mee-sohn*
stockings	**medias**	*mai-dee-ahs*
tights	**mallas**	*mah-Lahs*
gloves	**guantes**	*gw-ahn-tais*
handbag	**bolsa de mano**	*bohl-sah dai mah-noh*
shawl	**un chal**	*tshahl*
evening dress	**vestido de noche**	*vais-tee-doh dai noh-tshai*
Men's clothes	**ropa para hombres**	*roh-pah pah-rah ohm-brais*
shirt	**una camisa**	*oo-nah kah-mee-sah*
trousers	**pantalones**	*pahn-tah-loh-nais*
jacket	**una americana/ chaqueta**	*ah-mai-ree-kah-nah/ tshah-kai-tah*
suit	**un traje**	*trah-Gai*
umbrella	**un paraguas**	*pah-rah-gw-ahs*

handkerchief	**un pañuelo**	*pah-Noo-ai-loh*
pants	**calzoncillos**	*kahl-thohn-thee-Lohs*
vest	**una camiseta**	*kah-mee-sai-tah*
socks	**calcetines**	*kahl-thai-tee-nais*
pyjamas	**pijamas**	*pee-Gah-mahs*
tie	**una corbata**	*kohr-bah-tah*

Baby needs	**para niños**	*pah-rah nee-Nohs*

(generally available in the **droguería** or **farmacia**)

nappy	**un pañal**	*pah-Nahl*
feeding bottle	**un biberón**	*bee-bai-rohn*
teet	**una chupa**	*tshoo-pah*
baby food	**comida de niño**	*koh-mee-dah dai nee-Noh*

WEATHER AND TEMPERATURE

THE WEATHER	**el tiempo**	*tee-aim-poh*
The weather is fine (bad)	**hace buen (mal) tiempo**	*ah-thai boo-ain (mahl) tee-aim-poh*
it is hot	**hace calor**	*ah-thai kah-lohr*
it is cold	**hace frío**	*ah-thai free-oh*
it is cool	**está fresquito**	*ais-tah frais-kee-toh*
it is wet	**está lluvioso**	*ais-tah Loo-vee-oh-soh*
it is sunny	**hace sol**	*ah-thai sohl*
it is close	**está cargado**	*ais-tah kahr-gah-doh*
it is windy	**hace viento**	*ah-thai vee-ain-toh*
it is stormy	**va a caer una tormenta**	*vah ah kah-air oonah tohr-main-tah*
it is raining	**está lloviendo**	*aistah Loh-vee-ain-doh*
there is lightning	**hay relámpagos**	*ah-ee rai-lahm-pah-gohs*
there is thunder	**hay truenos**	*ah-ee troo-ai-nohs*

it is dull	**no hace sol**	*noh ah-thai sohl*
what's the weather like?	**¿qué tiempo hace?**	*kai tee-aim-poh ah-thai*
it's a terrible day	**hace un tiempo horrible**	*ah-thai oon tee-aim-poh oh-rree-blai*
it's a wonderful day	**hace muy buen tiempo**	*ah-thai moo-ee boo-ain tee-aim-poh*
it is going to rain	**va a llover**	*vah ah Loh-vair*
a rainbow	**un arco iris**	*oon ahr-koh ee-rees*
moon	**la luna**	*loo-nah*
stars	**las estrellas**	*ais-trai-Lahs*
barometer	**el barómetro**	*bah-roh-mai-troh*
thermometer	**el termómetro**	*tair-moh-mai-troh*
degree	**un grado**	*grah-doh*
I am cold (hot)	**tengo frío (calor)**	*tain-goh free-oh (kah-lohr)*
weather forecast	**el pronóstico del tiempo**	*proh-nohs-tee-koh dail tee-aim-poh*
is good (bad,) so-so	**está bueno (malo, regular)**	*aistah boo-ainoh (mah-loh, rai-goo-lahr)*

THE THERMOMETER	**el termómetro**	*tair-moh-mai-troh*

Fahrenheit	Centigrade
23	—5
32 freezing point	**—0 punto de congelación**
41	5
65	18.3
77	25
85	29.4
90	32.2
95	35
100	37.7
212 boiling point	**100 punto de ebullición**

Note: In Europe the Centigrade scale is used. To turn Fahrenheit into Centigrade, subtract 32 and multiply by 5/9 e.g.
77°F = (77 – 32) × 5/9 = 25°C.
To turn Centigrade into Fahrenheit, multiply by 9/5 and add 32, e.g.
5°C = (5 × 9/5) + 32 = 41°F.

TIME, DAYS, MONTHS AND SEASONS

DIVISIONS OF TIME

second	**un segundo**	*sai-goon-doh*
minute	**un minuto**	*mee-noo-toh*
Time of day	**la hora**	*lah oh-rah*
It is nearly 4.0 pm	**son casi las cuatro**	*sohn kah-see lahs koo-ahh-troh*
What time is it?	**¿qué hora es?**	*kai oh-rah ais*
it is exactly 2.0 pm	**son las dos en punto**	*sohn lahs dohs ain poon-toh*
it is about 3.0 pm	**son más o menos las tres**	*sohn mahs oh main-ohs lahs trais*
it is five past three	**son las tres y cinco**	*sohn lahs trais ee theen-koh*
it is a quarter past six	**son las seis y cuarto**	*sohn lahs sai-ees ee koo-ahr-toh*

it is half past seven	**son las siete y media**	*sohn lahs see-ai-tai ee mai-dee-ah*
it is twenty to eight	**son las ocho menos veinte**	*sohn lahs oh-tshoh mai-nohs vai-een-tai*
it is a quarter to ten	**son las diez menos cuarto**	*sohn lahs dee-aith mai-nohs koo-ahr-toh*
it is five to eleven	**son las once menos cinco**	*sohn lahs ohn-thai mai-nohs theen-koh*
it is midnight	**son las doce de la noche**	*sohn lahs doh-thai dai lah noh-tshai*
it is ten past midnight	**son las doce y diez de la noche**	*sohn lahs doh-thai ee dee-aith dai lah noh-tshai*
it is half past noon	**son las doce y media**	*sohn lahs do-thai ee mai-dee-ah*
shortly before (after) nine	**un poco antes (después) de las nueve**	*oon poh-koh ahn-tais (dais-poo-ais) dai lahs noo-ai-vai*
six a.m.	**las seis de la mañana**	*lahs sai-ees dai lah mah-Nah-nah*

ten p.m.	**las diez de la noche**	*sohn lahs dee-aith dai lah no-tshai*
towards 3 pm.	**cerca de las tres de la tarde**	*thair-kah dai lahs trais dai lah tahr-dai*
four in the morning	**las cuatro de la madrugada**	*lahs koo-ah-troh dai lah mah-droo-gah-dah*
eleven a.m.	**las once de la mañana**	*lahs ohn-thai dai lah mah-Nah-nah*
hour	**una hora**	*oh-rah*
half an hour	**media hora**	*mai-dee-ah oh-rah*
a quarter of an hour	**un cuarto de hora**	*koo-ahr-toh dai oh-rah*
day	**un día**	*dee-ah*
week	**una semana**	*sai-mah-nah*
fortnight	**una quincena**	*keen-thai-nah*
month	**un mes**	*mais*
year	**un año**	*ah-Noh*
sunrise	**la salida del sol**	*sah-lee-dah dail sohl*
dawn	**la aurora, la madrugada**	*ah-oo-roh-rah, mah-droo-gah-dah*
to get up early	**madrugar**	*mah-droo-gahr*

morning	**mañana**	*mah-Nah-Nah*
noon	**mediodía**	*mai-dee-oh-dee-ah*
afternoon/evening	**la tarde**	*tahr-dai*
night	**la noche**	*noh-tshai*
dusk	**el crepúsculo**	*krai-poos-koo-loh*
sunset	**la puesta del sol**	*poo-ais-tah dail sohl*
midnight	**medianoche**	*mai-dee-ah-noh-tshai*
A.M.	**ante meridiem**	*ahn-tai mai-ree-dee-aim*
P.M.	**post meridiem**	*pohst mai-ree-dee-aim*
during the day	**durante el día**	*doo-rahn-tai ail dee-ah*
The days of the week	**los días de la semana**	*dee-ahs dai lah sai-mah-mah*
Monday	**el lunes**	*loo-nais*
Tuesday	**el martes**	*mahr-tais*
Wednesday	**el miércoles**	*mee-air-koh-lais*
Thursday	**el jueves**	*Goo-ai-vais*
Friday	**el viernes**	*vee-air-nais*
Saturday	**el sábado**	*sah-bah-doh*
Sunday	**el domingo**	*doh-meen-goh*

Months of the year	**los meses del año**	*mai-sais dail ah-Noh*
January	**enero**	*ai-nai-roh*
February	**febrero**	*fai-brai-roh*
March	**marzo**	*mahr-thoh*
April	**abril**	*ah-breel*
May	**mayo**	*mah-yoh*
June	**junio**	*Goo-nee-oh*
July	**julio**	*Goo-lee-oh*
August	**agosto**	*ah-gohs-toh*
September	**septiembre**	*saip-tee-aim-brai*
October	**octubre**	*ohk-too-brai*
November	**noviembre**	*noh-vee-aim-brai*
December	**diciembre**	*dee-thee-aim-brai*

Note: The days of the week and months of the year are not capitalised, unless they come at the beginning of the sentence.

The seasons	**las estaciones**	*ais-tah-thee-oh-nais*
Spring	**la primavera**	*pree-mah-vai-rah*
Summer	**el verano**	*vai-rah-noh*
Autumn	**el otoño**	*oh-toh-Noh*
Winter	**el invierno**	*een-vee-air-noh*

what's the date today?	**¿qué día somos hoy?**	*kai dee-ah soh-mohs oh-ee*
the 1st of January	**el primero de enero**	*ail pree-mai-roh dai ain-ai-roh*
the 2nd of January	**el dos de enero**	*dohs dai ain-ai-roh*
the 3rd of January	**el tres de enero**	*trais dai ai-nai-roh*

PAST, PRESENT AND FUTURE

The past	**el pasado**	*ail pah-sah-doh*
yesterday	**ayer**	*ah-yair*
day before yesterday	**anteayer**	*ahn-tai-ah-yair*
a week ago today	**hoy hace una semana**	*oh-ee ah-thai oo-nah sai-mah-nah*
an hour ago	**hace una hora**	*ah-thai oo-nah oh-rah*
two days ago	**hace dos días**	*ah-thai dohs dee-ahs*
last Friday	**el viernes pasado**	*vee-air-nais pah-sah-doh*
last week	**la semana pasada**	*sai-mah-nah pah-sah-dah*
last night	**anoche**	*ah-noh-tshai*
this morning	**esta mañana**	*ais-tah mah-Nah-nah*
lately, recently	**últimamente, recientemente**	*ool-tee-mah-main-tai, rai-thee-ain-tai-main-tai*

a little while ago	**hace poco**	*ah-thai poh-koh*
just now	**ahora mismo**	*ah-oh-rah mees-moh*
The present	**el presente**	*prai-sain-tai*
today	**hoy**	*oh-ee*
now, at present	**ahora, al presente**	*ah-oh-rah, ahl-prai-sain-tai*
in time	**a tiempo**	*ah tee-aim-poh*
for the time being, temporarily	**provisionalmente**	*proh-vee-see-oh-nahl-main-tai*
The future	**el futuro**	*foo-too-roh*
tomorrow	**mañana**	*mah-Nah-nah*
tomorrow morning	**mañana por la mañana**	*mah-Nah-nah pohr lah mah-Nah-nah*
the day after tomorrow	**pasado mañana**	*pah-sah-doh mah-Nah-nah*
immediately	**en seguida, inmediatamente**	*ain sai-gee-dah, een-mai-dee-ah-tah-main-tai*

WHEN AND HOW OFTEN

soon	**pronto**	*prohn-toh*
directly	**directamente**	*dee-raik-tah-main-tai*
later on	**luego, más tarde**	*loo-ai-goh, mahs tahr-dai*
next week	**la semana que viene**	*sai-mah-nah kai vee-ain-ai*
this afternoon/ evening	**esta tarde**	*ais-tah tahr-dai*
tonight	**esta noche**	*ais-tah no-tshai*
in a short while	**en un rato**	*ain oon rah-toh*
within (after) five minutes	**dentro (después) de cinco minutos**	*dain-troh (dais-poo-ais) dai theen-koh mee-noo-tohs*
a long time	**mucho tiempo**	*moo-tshoh tee-aim-poh*
a short while	**un rato**	*oon rah-toh*

How often	**cuantas veces**	*koo-an-tahs vai-thais*
sometimes	**a veces**	*ah vai-thais*
often	**a menudo, muchas veces**	*ah mai-noo-doh, moo-tshahs vai-thais*
always	**siempre**	*see-aim-prai*
frequently	**con frecuencia**	*kohn frai-koo-ain-thee-ah*
constantly	**constantemente**	*kohn-stahn-tai-main-tai*
rarely	**pocas veces**	*poh-kahs vai-thais*
never	**nunca**	*noon-kah*
everyday	**cada día**	*kah-dah dee-ah*
twice a day	**dos veces al día**	*dohs vai-thaïs ahl dee-ah*
three times a week	**tres veces por semana**	*trais vai-thais pohr saim-ah-nah*
so often	**tantas veces**	*tahn-tahs vai-thais*
now and then	**de vez en cuando**	*dai vaith ain koo-ahn-doh*

THE FAMILY

The Family	**la familia**	*fah-mee-lee-ah*
christian name	**el nombre**	*nohm-brai*
surname	**el apellido**	*ah-pai-Lee-doh*
the parents	**los padres**	*pah-drais*
relatives	**los parientes**	*pah-ree-ain-tais*
father	**padre**	*pah-drai*
mother	**madre**	*mah-drai*
brother	**hermano**	*air-mah-noh*
sister	**hermana**	*air-mah-nah*
son	**hijo**	*ee-Goh*
daughter	**hija**	*ee-Gah*
parents-in-law	**suegros**	*soo-ai-grohs*
father-in-law	**suegro**	*soo-ai-groh*
mother-in-law	**suegra**	*soo-ai-grah*
sister-in-law	**cuñada**	*koo-Nah-dah*
brother-in-law	**cuñado**	*koo-Nah-doh*

son-in-law	**yerno**	*yair-noh*
daughter-in-law	**nuera**	*noo-ai-rah*
grandparents	**abuelos**	*ah-boo-ai-lohs*
grandfather	**abuelo**	*ah-boo-ai-loh*
grandmother	**abuela**	*ah-boo-ai-lah*
cousin (male)	**primo**	*pree-moh*
cousin (female)	**prima**	*pree-mah*
uncle	**tío**	*tee-oh*
aunt	**tía**	*tee-ah*
nephew	**sobrino**	*soh-bree-noh*
niece	**sobrina**	*soh-bree-nah*
born	**nacido**	*nah-thee-doh*
birth	**nacimiento**	*nah-thee-mee-ain-toh*
birthday	**cumpleaños**	*koohm-plai-ah-Nohs*
by birth	**de origen**	*dai oh-ree-Gain*
godfather	**padrino**	*pah-dree-noh*
godmother	**madrina**	*mah-dree-nah*
godson/daughter	**ahijado/a**	*ah-ee-Gah-doh/ah*
baby	**un bebe**	*bai-bai*
a small boy	**niño**	*nee-Noh*
a small girl	**niña**	*nee-Nah*

a young man	**un chico**	*tshee-koh*
a young woman	**una chica**	*tshee-kah*
unmarried	**soltero/a**	*sohl-tai-roh/ah*
engaged	**novio/a**	*noh-vee-oh/ah*
married	**casado/a**	*kah-sah-doh/ah*
husband	**marido**	*mah-ree-doh*
wife	**esposa**	*ais-poh-sah*

THE BODY

The Body	el cuerpo	*koo-air-poh*
head	la cabeza	*kah-bai-thah*
forehead	la frente	*frain-tai*
face	la cara	*kah-rah*
ear	la oreja	*oh-rai-Gah*
eye	el ojo	*oh-Goh*
eyebrow	la ceja	*thai-Gah*
eyelash	la pestaña	*pais-tah-Nah*
eyelid	el párpado	*pahr-pah-doh*
nose	la naríz	*nah-reeth*
mouth	la boca	*boh-kah*
tongue	la lengua	*lain-gw-ah*
lip	el labio	*lah-bee-oh*
cheek	la mejilla	*mai-Gee-Lah*
skin	la piel	*pee-ail*
chin	el mentón	*main-tohn*
beard	la barba	*bahr-bah*

moustache	**el bigote**	*bee-goh-tai*
neck	**el cuello**	*koo-ai-Loh*
shoulder	**el hombro**	*ohm-broh*
chest, breast	**el pecho**	*pai-tshoh*
heart	**el corazón**	*koh-rah-thohn*
arm	**el brazo**	*brah-thoh*
elbow	**el codo**	*koh-doh*
stomach	**el estómago**	*aistoh-mah-goh*
back	**la espalda**	*ais-pahl-dah*
hand	**la mano**	*mah-noh*
thumb	**el pulgar**	*pool-gahr*
finger	**el dedo**	*dai-doh*
waist	**la cintura**	*theen-too-rah*
leg	**la pierna**	*pee-air-nah*
knee	**la rodilla**	*roh-dee-Lah*
foot	**el pie**	*pee-ai*
toe	**el dedo del pie**	*dai-doh dail pee-ai*
blood	**la sangre**	*sahn-grai*
bald	**calvo**	*kahl-voh*
blind	**ciego**	*thee-ai-goh*
deaf	**sordo**	*sohr-doh*
dumb	**mudo**	*moo-doh*

crippled	lisiado	*lee-see-ah-doh*
slim	delgado	*dail-gah-doh*
stout	gordo	*gohr-doh*
young	joven	*Goh-vain*
old	viejo	*vee-ai-Goh*
tall	alto	*ahl-toh*
small	bajo	*bah-Goh*
middlesized	de talla normal	*dai tah-Lah nohr-mahl*
she has a nice figure	tiene una forma bonita	*tee-ai-nai oonah fohr-mah boh-nee-tah*
good looking	guapo	*goo-ah-poh*
bless you! (to someone sneezing)	¡Jesús!	*Gai-soos*
voice	la voz	*voh-th*
to speak	hablar	*ah-blahr*
to whisper	susurrar	*soo-soo-rrahr*
to call	llamar	*Lah-mahr*
to shout	gritar	*gree-tahr*
to cry	llorar	*Loh-rahr*
to sing	cantar	*kahn-tahr*
to swallow	tragar	*trah-gahr*
to breathe	respirar	*rais-pee-rahr*

HEALTH

Health	**la salud**	*sah-lood*
how are you?	**¿cómo está usted?**	*koh-moh ais-tah oos-taid*
	¿qué tál está usted?	*kai-tahl ais-tah oos-taid*
how is your father?	**¿cómo está su padre?**	*koh-moh ais-tah soo pah-drai*
very well, thank you	**muy bien, gracias**	*moo-ee bee-ain grah-thee-ahs*
quite well	**regular**	*rai-goo-lahr*
not too well	**no muy bien**	*noh-moo-ee bee-ain*
you look well	**usted parece bien**	*oos-taid pah-rai-thai bee-ain*
are you not well?	**¿no se encuentra bien?**	*noh sai ain-koo-ain-trah bee-ain*
what is the matter with you?	**¿qué le pasa a usted?**	*kai lai pah-sah ah oos-taid*
I don't know	**no sé**	*noh sai*

SPORT

Sport	**los deportes**	*dai-pohr-tais*
to play tennis (golf, football)	**jugar al tenis (golf, fútbol)**	*Goo-gahr ahl tai-nees (gohlf, foot-bohl)*
a game of	**un partido de**	*oon pahr-tee-doh dai*
team	**el equipo**	*ai-kee-poh*
event; race meeting	**un encuentro**	*ain-koo-ain-troh*
heat	**la carrera eliminatoria**	*kah-rrai-rah ai-lee-mee-nah-toh-ree-ah*
semi-final	**la semifinal**	*sai-mee-fee-nahl*
final	**la final**	*fee-nahl*
half time	**medio-tiempo**	*mai-dee-oh tee-aim-poh*
second-half	**la segunda parte**	*sai-goon-dah pahr-tai*
referee	**el árbitro**	*ahr-bee-troh*
spectator	**el espectador**	*ais-paik-tah-dohr*
ground	**el campo**	*kahm-poh*
stadium	**el estadio**	*ais-tah-dee-oh*

handicap	**el hándicap**	*ahn-dee-kahp*
penalty	**una sanción**	*sahn-thee-ohn*
to disqualify	**descalificar**	*dais-kah-lee-fee-kahr*
to beat	**ganar a**	*gah-nahr ah*
to win (won)	**ganar (ganado)**	*gah-nahr (gah-nah-doh)*
to lose (lost)	**perder (perdido)**	*pair-dair (pair-dee-doh)*
athletics	**el atletismo**	*ah-tlai-tees-moh*
to run	**correr**	*koh-rrair*
to jump	**saltar**	*sahl-tahr*
Boating	**la náutica**	*nah-oo-tee-kah*
rowing boat	**barco de remo**	*bahr-koh da rai-moh*
sailing boat	**barco de vela**	*bahr-koh dai vai-lah*
oars	**remos**	*rai-mohs*
sails	**velas**	*vai-lahs*
starboard	**estribor**	*ais-tree-bohr*
port	**babor**	*bah-bohr*
compass	**brújula**	*broo-Goo-lah*
rocks	**las rocas**	*roh-kahs*

outboard motor boat	**una fuera-borda**	*foo-ai-rah bohr-dah*
outboard motor	**un motor fuere de borda**	*moh-toh foo-air-rai dai bohr-dah*
water skiing	**esquí náutico**	*ais-kee nah-oo-tee-koh*
water polo	**water-polo**	*wah-tair-poh-loh*
surfing	**surfing**	*soor-feeng*
surfboard	**patín de mar**	*pah-teen dai mahr*
sandbank	**banco de arena**	*bahn-koh dai ah-rai-nah*
sandbar	**barra de arena**	*bah-rrah dai ah-rai-nah*
Cycling	**el ciclismo**	*thee-clees-moh*
to cycle	**montar en bicicleta**	*mohn-tahr ain bee-thee-clai-tah*
to peddle	**pedalear**	*pai-dah-lai-ahr*
Fishing	**la pesca**	*pais-kah*
to fish	**pescar**	*pais-kahr*
angling	**pescar con caña**	*pais-kahr kohn kah-Nah*
fishing rod	**caña (de pescar)**	*cah-Nah (dai pais-kahr)*

line	**el sedal**	*sai-dahl*
fish hook	**el anzuelo**	*ahn-thoo-ai-loh*
bait	**carnada**	*kahr-nah-dah*
Football	**el fútbol**	*foot-bohl*
players	**los jugadores**	*Goo-gah-doh-rais*
goal	**el gol**	*gohl*
goal keeper	**el guardameta**	*goo-ahr-dah-mai-tah*
a pass	**un pase**	*pah-sai*
to tackle	**blocar al jugador**	*blok-ah ahl Goo-gah-dohr*
a free kick	**un saque libre**	*sah-kai lee-brai*
to throw in	**tirar la pelota**	*tee-rahr lah pai-loh-tah*
to be off-side	**estar en 'off-side'**	*ais-tahr ain* (same as English)
to dribble	**driblar**	*dree-blahr*
to shoot	**chutar**	*tshoo-tahr*
shooter	**el tirador**	*tee-rah-dohr*
Game Shooting	**la caza**	*kah-thah*
gun	**el fusil**	*foo-seel*

cartridge	**el cartucho**	*kahr-too-tshoh*
bullet	**la bala**	*bah-lah*
Golf	**el golf**	*gohlf*
golf course	**campo de golf**	*kahm-poh dai gohlf*
golf club (stick)	**palo de golf**	*pah-loh dai gohlf*
Horse Racing	**hipódromo**	*hee-poh-droh-moh*
race course	**pista de carreras**	*pees-tah dai kah-rrai-rahs*
a race	**una carrera**	*kah-rrai-rah*
an obstacle race	**carrera de obstáculos**	*kah-rrai-rah dai ohbs-tah-koo-lohs*
a steeplechase	**carrera através del campo**	*kah-rrai-rah ah-trah-vais dail kahm-poh*
the stands	**las tribunas**	*tree-boon-ahs*
starting point	**punto de partida**	*poon-toh dai pahr-tee-dah*
finish	**la meta**	*mai-tah*
winner	**el ganador**	*gah-nah-dohr*
to bet	**apostar**	*ah-pohs-tahr*

bookmaker	**corredor de apuestas**	*koh-rrai-dohr dai ah-poo-ais-tahs*
to ride	**montar a caballo**	*mohn-tahr ah kah-bah-Loh*
Skating	**el patinaje**	*pah-tee-nah-Gai*
to skate	**patinar**	*pah-tee-nahr*
ice skating	**patinaje sobre hielo**	*pah-tee-nah-Gai soh-brai ee-ai-loh*
roller skating	**patinaje sobre ruedas**	*pah-tee-nah-Gai soh-brai roo-ai-dahs*
a skate	**un patín**	*pah-teen*
skating rink	**pista de patinar**	*peestah dai pah-tee-nahr*
Ski-ing	**el esquí**	*ais-kee*
skis	**los esquís**	*ais-kees*
ski boots	**botas de esquí**	*boh-tahs dai ais-kee*
ski stick	**bastón de esquí**	*bahs-ton dai ais-kee*
ski lift	**tele-esquí**	*tai-lai-ais-kee*
beginner' slopes	**pista de principiantes**	*pees-tah dai pree-thee pee-ahn-tais*

advanced slope	**pista de avanzados**	*pees-tah dai ah-vahn-thah-dohs*
toboggan	**un tobogán**	*toh-boh-gahn*
ski jump	**salto de esquí**	*sahl-toh dai ais-kee*
Swimming	**la natación**	*nah-tah-thee-ohn*
to swim	**nadar**	*nah-dahr*
swimming pool	**la piscina**	*pees-thee-nah*
diving board	**el trampolín**	*trahm-poh-leen*
to dive	**saltar desde el trampolín**	*sahl-tahr dais-dai ail trahm-poh-leen*
to dive (underwater)	**bucear**	*boo-thai-ahr*
Tennis	**el tenis**	*tai-nees*
tennis court	**campo de tenis**	*kahm-poh dai tai-nees*
racket	**la raqueta**	*rah-kai-tah*
ball	**la pelota**	*pai-loh-tah*
net	**la red**	*raid*
to serve/service	**sacar/saque**	*sah-kahr/sah-kai*
tournament	**el torneo**	*tohr-nai-oh*

BULLFIGHTING

Bullfighting	**los toros**	*toh-rohs*
bull ring	**la plaza de toros**	*plah-thah dai toh-rohs*
ticket	**la entrada**	*ain-trah-dah*
row of seats	**el tendido**	*tain-dee-doh*
bull	**el toro**	*toh-roh*
the horses	**los caballos**	*kah-bah-Lohs*
the bull fighters	**los toreros**	*toh-rai-rohs*
the ground dart throwers	**los banderilleros**	*bahn-dai-ree-Lai-rohs*
the mounted dart throwers	**los picadores**	*pee-kah-doh-rais*
matador	**el matador**	*mah-tah-dohr*
the capes (used by the 'toreros')	**los capotes**	*kah-poh-tais*
the red cape (used by the 'matador')	**la muleta**	*moo-lai-tah*
the killer sword	**el estoque**	*ais-toh-kai*
the president's chair	**la presidencia**	*prai-see-dain-thee-ah*
the barrier	**la barrera**	*bah-rrai-rah*

ENTERTAINMENTS

Entertainments	**los espectaculos**	*ais-paik-tah-koo-lohs*
theatre	**un teatro**	*tai-ah-troh*
opera	**una ópera**	*oh-pai-rah*
musical comedy	**una zarzuela**	*thahr-thoo-ai-lah*
a comedy	**una comedia**	*koh-mai-dee-ah*
concert	**un concierto**	*kohn-thee-air-toh*
orchestra	**una orquesta**	*ohr-kais-tah*
cinema	**un cine**	*thee-nai*
box office	**la taquilla**	*tah-kee-Lah*
to book a seat	**reservar plazas**	*rai-sair-vahr plah-thahs*
ticket	**una entrada**	*ain-trah-dah*
programme	**el programa**	*proh-grah-mah*
opera glasses	**gemelos de teatro**	*Gai-mai-lohs dai tai-ah-troh*
a box	**un palco**	*pahl-koh*

dress circle seats	**butacas del primer piso**	*boo-tah-kahs dail pree-mair pee-soh*
the gallery	**el anfiteatro**	*ahn-fee-tai-ah-troh*
the stalls	**salón de butaca**	*sah-lohn dai boo-tah-kah*
the pit	**el foso**	*foh-soh*
interval	**entreacto**	*ain-trai-ahk-toh*
an act	**un acto**	*ahk-toh*
the stage	**el escenario**	*ais-thai-nah-ree-oh*
the curtain	**el telón**	*tai-lohn*
the screen	**la pantalla**	*pahn-tah-Lah*
toilets	**los servicios**	*sair-vee-thee-ohs*
cloakroom	**guardaropa**	*goo-ahr-dah-roh-pah*
Dancing	**el baile**	*bah-ee-lai*
to dance	**bailar**	*bah-ee-lahr*
a discotheque	**una discoteca**	*dees-koh-tai-kah*
a dance hall	**salón de baile**	*sah-lohn dai bah-ee-lai*
records	**discos**	*dees-kohs*
a group	**un conjunto**	*kohn-Goon-toh*
a band	**una banda**	*bahn-dah*

GAMES AND PASTIMES

Pastimes	pasatiempos	*pah-sah-tee-aim-pohs*
do you like . . . ?	¿le gusta . . . ?	*lai goos-tah*
music (modern or classical)	la música (moderna o clásica)	*moo-see-kah (moh-dair-nah oh klah-see-kah)*
singing	cantar	*kahn-tahr*
painting	pintar	*peen-tahr*
drawing	dibujar	*dee-boo-Gahr*
sculpture	esculpir	*ais-kool-peer*
skating	patinar	*pah-tee-nahr*
dancing	bailar	*bah-ee-lahr*
the radio	la radio	*rah-dee-oh*
the television	la televisión	*tai-lai-vee-see-ohn*
walking	caminar	*kah-mee-nahr*
bull fighting	las corridas de toros	*lahs koh-rree-dahs dai toh-rrohs*

do you play the piano?	¿toca el piano?	*toh-kah ai! pee-ah-noh*
do you play the guitar?	¿toca la guitarra?	*toh-kah lah gee-tah-rrah*
do you play cards?	¿juega a las cartas?	*Goo-ai-gah ah lahs kahr-tahs*
do you play chess?	¿juega al ajedrez?	*Goo-ai-gah aht ah-Gai-draith*
do you play billiards?	¿juega al billar?	*Goo-ai-gah ahl bee-Lahr*
do you play draughts?	¿juega a las damas?	*Goo-ai-gah ahlahs dah-mahs*
A Game of Chess	un partido de ajedrez	*oon pahr-tee-doh dai ah-Gai-draith*
chessboard	tablero de ajedrez	*tah-blai-roh dai ah-Gai-draith*
king	el rey	*rai-ee*
queen	la reina	*rai-ee-nah*
knight	el caballo	*kah-bah-Loh*
castle	la torre	*toh-rrai*

bishop	**el alfil**	*ahl-feel*
pawn	**el peón**	*pai-ohn*
to castle	**enrocar**	*ain-roh-kahr*
check (to the king)	**jaque**	*Gah-kai*
checkmate	**jaque mate**	*Gah-kai mah-tai*
Billiards	**billar**	*bee-Lahr*
billiard table	**mesa de billar**	*mai-sah dai bee-Lahr*
a cue	**el taco**	*tah-koh*
ball	**la bola**	*boh-lah*
cushion	**la baranda**	*bah-rahn-dah*
to cannon	**carambolear**	*kah-rahm-boh-lai-ahr*
Cards	**las cartas**	*kahr-tahs*
what games do you play?	**¿a qué juega usted?**	*ah kai Goo-ai-gah oos-taid*
bridge	**al bridge**	*ahl* (as in English)
poker	**al pocker**	*ahl* (as in English)
to play patience	***hacer un solitario**	*ah-thair oon soh-lee-tah-ree-oh*
a suit	**un palo**	*pah-loh*

hearts	**corazón**	*koh-rah-thohn*
diamonds	**diamantes**	*dee-ah-mahn-tais*
clubs	**tréboles**	*trai-boh-lais*
spades	**picas**	*pee-kahs*
the queen	**la dama**	*dah-mah*
the king	**el rey**	*rai-ee*
the jack	**el caballo**	*kah-bah-Loh*
to follow suit	**servir del palo**	*sair-veer dail pah-loh*
to shuffle	**barajar**	*bah-rah-Gahr*
to cut	**cortar**	*kohr-tahr*
whose deal?	**¿quién da?**	*kee-ain dah*
whose lead?	**¿quién juega?**	*kee-ain Goo-ai-gah*
whose turn?	**¿a quién toca?**	*ah kee-ain toh-kah*

Note: Spanish playing cards differ entirely from British both in number and in suits, however the 53 pack playing cards are well known and commonly used.

RADIO AND TELEVISION

Radio and television	**la radio y la televisión**	*rah-dee-oh ee tai-lai-vee see-ohn*
transistor radio	**radio transistor**	*rah-dee-oh trahn-sees-tohr*
a programme	**un programa**	*proh-grah-mah*
loud speaker	**un altavoz**	*ahl-tah-vohth*
an aerial	**una antena**	*ahn-tai-nah*
VHF	**frecuencia modulada (FM)**	*frai-koo-ain-thee-ah moh-doo-lah-dah*
LW	**onda larga**	*ohn-dah lahr-gah*
SW	**onda corta**	*ohn-dah kohr-tah*
to listen in	**escuchar la radio**	*ais-koo-tshahr lah rah-dee-oh*
to switch on	**poner la radio**	*poh-nair lah rah-dee-oh*
to switch off	**apagar la radio**	*ah-pah-gahr lah rah-dee-oh*
channel	**un canal**	*kah-nahl*

LETTER WRITING

Date – top right hand corner, preceded by the name of town or place you are writing from.

Address – On the back of the envelope, except in business letters when it is placed on the left above the salutation.

Both the beginnings and endings of Spanish letters are very much more elaborate and varied than the English style, and so the following are only some of the possiblities. **s.s.=seguro servidor**, and is usually abbreviated.

Starting a letter

1) business letter
   e.g. Dear Sir/Madam – **señor/señora**
2) business letter
   e.g. Dear Mr. . . . – **Muy señor mío**

Ending a letter

1) yours faithfully – **Suyo atentísimo**
2) Best wishes, yours sincerely, – **Suyo afectisímo, su s.s.**

3) business friend or formal acquaintance on christian name terms – **Muy señor mio y amigo**

4) to good friends e.g. Dear Mary/Peter – **Querida/o María/Pedro**

3) Kind regards, – **Con el mayor afecto, su s.s.**

4) fond regards, love from . . . – **Muchos recuerdos, un abrazo**

Dear sir,

Please could you advise me by return, the price of a SINGLE ROOM, TWIN BEDDED ROOM, DOUBLE BEDDED ROOM with/without bathroom.

Yours faithfully,

Señor.,

Tenga la bondad de deçirme a vuelta de correos, el precio de una habitación INDIVIDUAL, CON DOS CAMAS, CON CAMA DE MATRIMONIO, con/sin cuarto de baño.

Suyo atentísimo,

Dear Sir,

Wouid you please be kind enough to send me a brochure about your camping site, with particular reference to washing and bathing facilities.

Hoping for a speedy reply,

Yours faithfully,

Señor.,

Haga el favor de mandarme un folleto de su 'camping' – con informaciones particularmente de las facilidades higiénicas y de natición.

Esperando una rápida contestación,

Suyo afectísimo,

Dear Sir,

Please could you let me know the price of a double room with bathroom, and an adjoining twin bedded room. All with FULL/HALF BOARD. Do you have any price reductions for children?

Yours faithfully,

Señor.,

Tenga la amibilidad de decirme que precio tienen ustedes para una habitación de matrimonio con baño y con comunicación a otra habitación de dos camas. Todos con PENSION COMPLETA/MEDIA PENSION. ¿Tienen ustedes un precio especial para niños?

Su seguro servidor,

Dear Sir,

Please reserve me a single room from the 3rd of July to the 16th July inclusive.

Yours faithfully,

Señor.,

Reserveme por favor, una habitación individual para el 3 de julio hasta el 16 del mismo incluido.

Suyo atentísimo,

EMERGENCY – ILLNESS OR ACCIDENT

EMERGENCY	EMERGENCIA	*ai-mair-Gain-thee-ah*
Aches and Pains	**dolores**	*doh-loh-rais*
headache	**dolar de cabeza**	*doh-lohr dai kah-bai-thah*
stomach ache	**dolor de estómago**	*doh-lohr dai ais-toh-mah-goh*
sore throat	**dolor de garganta**	*doh-lohr dai-gahr-gahn-tah*
toothache	**dolor de muelas**	*doh-lohr dai moo-ai-lahs*
earache	**dolor de oído**	*doh-lohr dai oh-ee-doh*
backache	**dolor de espalda**	*doh-lohr dai ais-pahl-dah*
I have a pain here	**tengo un dolor aquí**	*tain-goh oon doh-lohr ah-kee*

Illness	**enfermedad**	*ain-fair-mai-dahd*
I am ill	**estoy enfermo/a**	*ais-toh-ee ain-fair-moh/ah*
he has a temperature	**tiene fiebre**	*tee-ai-nai fee-ai-brai*
he feels dizzy	**siente mareo**	*see-ain-tai mah-rai-oh*
he has fainted	**se ha desmayado**	*sai ah dais-mah-yah-doh*
he is vomiting	**está devolviendo**	*ais-tah dai-vohl-vee-ain-doh*
he has a cold	**está costipado**	*ais-tah kohs-tee-pah-doh*
appendicitis	**apendicitis**	*ah-pain-dee-thee-tees*
heart attack	**un ataque cardíaco**	*oon ah-tah-kai kahr-dee-ah-koh*
he has taken an over-dose of . . .	**ha tomado una dosis excesiva de . . .**	*ah toh-mah-doh oo-nah doh-sees aix-thai-see-vah dai . .*
he has diarrhoea	**tiene diarrea**	*tee-ai-nai dee-ah-rai-ah*
Accidents on Land	**accidentes sobre tierra**	*ank-thee-dain-tais soh-brai tee-ai-rrah*

there has been a (car, bus, train, plane) accident	**ha habido un accidente (de coche, autobus, tren, avión)**	*ah ah-bee-doh oon ahk-thee-dain-tai (dai koh-tshai ah-oo-toh-boos, train, ah-vee-ohn)*
three people are injured	**hay tres heridos**	*ah-ee trais ai-ree-dohs*
some cuts and bruises	**unos rasguños y contusíones**	*oo-nohs rahs-goo-Nohs ee kohn-too-see-ohn-ais*
he has hurt his leg	**se ha hecho daño en la pierna**	*sai ah ai-tshoh dah-Noh ain lah pee-air-nah*
he has broken his arm	**se rompió el brazo**	*sai rohm-pee-oh ail brah-thoh*
he has sprained his ankle	**se ha doblado el tobillo**	*sai ah doh-blah-doh ail toh-bee-Loh*
he has been knocked over by a car	**le cogió un coche**	*lai koh-Gee-oh oon koh-tshai*
he has fallen off the rocks	**se ha caído de las rocas**	*sai ah kah-ee-doh dai lahs roh-kahs*

he is unconscious	**está inconsciente**	*ais-tah een-kohns-thee-ain-tai*
he has had an electric shock	**ha recibido una descarga eléctrica**	*ah rai-thee-bee-do oon-ah kahr-gah ai-laik-tree-kah*
he has been poisoned with this	**ha sido envenenado con esto**	*ah ais-tah-doh ain-vai-nai-nah-doh kohn ais-toh*
there is a fire	**hay un incendio**	*ah-ee oon een-thain-dee-oh*
there is an avalanche	**hay una avalancha**	*ah-ee oon-ah ah-vah-lahn-tshah*
I have been robbed	**he sido robado**	*ai see-doh roh-bah-doh*
At Sea	**en el mar**	*ain ail mahr*
man overboard!	**¡un hombre en el agua!**	*oon ohm-brai ain ail ah-goo-ah*
he cannot swim	**no puede nadar**	*noh poo-ai-dai nah-dahr*
he is drowning	**está ahogándose**	*ais-tah ah-oh-gahn-doh-sai*

the boat has capsized	**el barco ha zozobrado**	*ail bahr-koh ah thoh-thoh-brah-doh*
the boat has sunk	**el barco se ha hundido**	*ail bahr-koh sai ah oon-dee-doh*
the boat has hit the rocks	**se ha dado con las rocas**	*sai ah dah-doh kohn lahs roh-kahs*
he has got cramp	**tiene un calambre**	*tee-ai-nai oon kah-lahm-brai*
he is being swept out to sea	**el mar lo está llevando**	*ail mahr loh ais-tah Lai-vahn-doh*
do you know artificial respiration?	**¿sabe usted hacer la respiración artificial?**	*sah-bai oos-taid ah-thair lah rais-pee-rah-thee-ohn ahr-tee-fee-thee-ahl*
General	**en general**	*ain Gai-nai-rahl*
a pain	**un dolor**	*doh-lohr*
it is bleeding	**está sangrando**	*ais-tah san-gran-doh*
wounded	**herido**	*ai-ree-doh*
swollen	**hinchado(a)**	*intsh-ah-doh*
burnt	**quemado**	*kai-mah-doh*

bruised	**cardenal**	*kahr-dai-nahl*
a bandage	**una venda**	*vain-dah*
a plaster	**un esparadrapo**	*ais-pah-rah-drah-poh*
doctor	**un médico**	*mai-dee-koh*
nurse	**una enfermera**	*ain-fair-mai-rah*
dentist	**un dentista**	*dain-tees-tah*
tooth	**el diente**	*dee-ain-tai*
to fill	**empastar**	*aim-pahs-tahr*
to take out	**sacar**	*sah-kahr*
my blood group is O, A, AB	**mi grupo de sangre es O, A, AB**	*mee groo-poh dai sahn-grai ais oh, ah, ah-bai*
I am allergic to penicillin	**tengo alergia a la penicilina**	*tain-goh ah-lair-Gee-ah ah lah pai-nee-thee-lee-nah*
I am allergic to dust	**tengo alergia al polvo**	*tain-goh ahl-air-Gee-ah ahl pohl-voh*

CALLING FOR HELP

Calling for help	**pedir ayuda**	*pai-deer ah-yoo-dah*
help!, help!	**¡socorro! ¡socorro!**	*soh-koh-rroh*
please call for a doctor	**por favor llame al médico**	*pohr fah-vohr Lah-mai ahl mai-dee-koh*
please call for an ambulance	**por favor, pida una ambulancia**	*pohr fah-vohr pee-dah oo-nah ahm-boo-lahn-thee-ah*
please call out a search party	**por favor reuna un grupo de gente para buscarle**	*pohr fah-vohr rai-oo-nah oon groo-poh dai Gain-tai pah-rah boos-kahr-lai*
call the fire brigade	**¡llamé a los bomberos!**	*Lah-mai ah lohs bohm-bai-rohs*
call the lifeboat!	**¡llame al barco de socorro!**	*La-mai ahl bahr-koh dai soh-koh-rroh*
call the life guard!	**¡llame al socorrista!**	*Lah-mai ahl soh-koh-rrees-tah*

call the police!	**¡llame a la policía!**	*Lah-mai ah lah poh-lee-thee-ah*
where is the nearest hospital (doctor, dentist, police station)?	**¿dondé está el hospital (médico, dentista, la comisaría de policía) más cercá?**	*dohn-dai ais-tah ail ohs-pee-tahl (mai-dee-koh, dain-tees-tah, lah koh-mee-sah-ree-ah dai poh-lee-thee-ah) mahs thair-kah*
my wife is pregnant	**mi señora está embarazada**	*mee sai-Noh-rah ais-tah aim-bah-rah-thah-dah*
her time has come	**ha llegado su hora**	*ah Lai-gah-doh soo oh-rah*

SOS BY PUBLIC TELEPHONE

There is no emergency telephone number in Spain to correspond to the British '999'. Each town has its own series of emergency telephone numbers for police, fire station, doctor, ambulance, which are placed in public telephone boxes, and on the front page of the telephone directories.

THE SUNSHINE PHRASE BOOKS

Uniform with this book

Sunshine German Phrase Book

Sunshine French Phrase Book

Sunshine Italian Phrase Book

Sunshine Spanish Phrase Book

Some paperfronts are listed on the following pages. A full list of the titles currently available can be had by sending a stamped addressed envelope to:

Elliot Right Way Books, Lower Kingswood, Tadworth, Surrey, U.K.

Some other Paperfronts:

Healthy Houseplants A–Z
Out Of The Freezer Into The Microwave
Microwave Cooking Properly Explained
Food Processors Properly Explained
Slow Cooking Properly Explained
Wine Making The Natural Way
Easymade Wine
Traditional Beer And Cider Making
Handbook Of Herbs
Buying Or Selling A House

Elliot Right Way Books, Kingswood, Surrey, U.K.

Some other Paperfronts:

Highway Code Questions And Answers
Car Driving In Two Weeks
Learning To Drive In Pictures
Pass Your Motor-cycle L Test
Car Repairs Properly Explained
Car Doctor A–Z
Begin Chess
Right Way To Play Chess
Begin Bridge
The Knot Book

Elliot Right Way Books, Kingswood, Surrey, U.K.